Financial Incentives for Employees

Paul Roots

formerly Director of Industrial Relations,
Ford Motor Co Ltd

BSP PROFESSIONAL BOOKS
OXFORD LONDON EDINBURGH
BOSTON PALO ALTO MELBOURNE

First published 1988

British Library
Cataloguing in Publication Data
Roots, Paul
Financial incentives for employees.
1. Great Britain. Personnel.
Remuneration.
Incentive schemes
I. Title
331.2'164'0941

ISBN 0-632-01925-5

BSP Professional Books
A division of Blackwell Scientific Publications Ltd
Editorial Offices:
Osney Mead, Oxford OX2 0EL
(Orders: Tel. 0865 240201)
8 John Street, London WC1N 2ES
23 Ainslie Place, Edinburgh EH3 6AJ
3 Cambridge Center, Suite 208, Cambridge, MA 02142, USA
667 Lytton Avenue, Palo Alto, California 94301, USA
107 Barry Street, Carlton, Victoria 3053, Australia

Set by Setrite Typesetters Ltd
Printed and bound in Great Britain by Mackays of Chatham PLC, Chatham, Kent

Contents

Preface *v*

1 Why Use Financial Incentives? 1

2 The Arguments For And Against Financial Incentives 11

3 The Essential Ingredients For The Successful Use Of Financial Incentives 20

4 The Choice Of Schemes Available 33

5 Profit-sharing And Employee Shareholding 51

6 Communicating, Negotiating And Introducing Financial Incentives 62

7 Implementation And Monitoring The Results 87

8 What To Do If It Goes Wrong 93

9 Productivity Bargaining 103

10 Pay Strategy 130

Appendix I: Management Check List 145

Appendix II:	**An Added Value Bonus Scheme**	**147**
Appendix III:	**BAT Industries PLC Save-As-You-Earn Share Option Scheme**	**150**
Appendix IV:	**Reed International UK and Overseas Executive Share Option Schemes (1984)**	**159**
Appendix V:	**A Production-related Bonus Scheme**	**164**
Index		**169**

Preface

With few exceptions people work to earn money. Does this mean that they will work harder, better, more regularly for more money? Every director, manager, supervisor, trade union official and shop steward knows life is not that simple. Human behaviour and what motivates it is a complex subject, and many books have been written by psychologists, sociologists and management specialists explaining why and in what circumstances other factors take precedence over money in the work situation.

This book does not enter into these areas except where it is necessary to illustrate a point. It is designed to explain some of the ways in which money can be used to influence employees so that those considering introducing such methods will be aware of the schemes which are available and their advantages and disadvantages. It deals with financial incentives to increase performance, improve attendance, reduce employee turnover and improve labour flexibility. It includes on-going payments such as individual and group payment by results schemes, and one-off payments of the type used in what is now known as productivity bargaining.

I am indebted to all my old friends and colleagues in industry, the Institute of Personnel Management and the Confederation of British Industry who provided me with background information, and especially grateful to BAT Industries and Reed International for permitting me to include descriptions of their Share Option Schemes. I also wish to thank Ron Todd, General Secretary of the Transport and General Workers Union for permission to reproduce an extract from their book *Plant Level Bargaining*.

It is hoped that this book will help managers and others to avoid some of the less obvious hazards in what can be an aid to higher productivity or an employee relations minefield.

Paul Roots
1988

Chapter 1

Why Use Financial Incentives?

1.01 Introduction

Financial incentives have a long history and references can be found to payment by results in the Old Testament, Shakespeare and the writings of the Ancient Greeks. In Britain, when paid employment, as distinct from service, increased in the sixteenth and seventeenth centuries, the wages, which were often regulated by Act of Parliament and Justices of the Peace, were normally piece-rate.

Although there are no precise figures available, and the popularity of financial incentive schemes ebbs and flows, it is estimated that upwards of 40 per cent of employees in Britain have some part of their pay linked to performance. In the engineering industry it is closer to 50 per cent.

The last survey published in the United States showed that 59 per cent of the companies surveyed used incentives, and even some communist countries make use of piece-work and bonuses. In Japan the majority of workers rely on bonuses for, on average, 20 per cent of their wages. There are, however, successful companies which do not use any form of direct financial incentive, and rely on trained supervision combined with well maintained facilities and systems to provide a constant work effort.

In recent years there has been increased management interest in employee participation and motivating employees by involving them more in the problems which affect the business. Sometimes, but not always, this approach is combined with financial participation in the company's fortunes by means of profit sharing or employee shareholding schemes.

1.02 The role of pay

Most organisations exist to provide goods or services at a profit. Management's job is to plan and implement policies which make that happen. It follows, therefore, that pay policy, and indeed all personnel policies, should be designed with one main objective – to enable the organisation to recruit, retain and motivate sufficient people of the right skills and abilities to meet its profit target.

Recruiting the necessary number of people with the appropriate skills is the determining factor when it comes to the level of pay offered. Pay is the biggest single reason why people change jobs and, therefore, it is the primary attraction for those seeking work. The level of pay on offer also says something to the prospective applicant about the company. Organisations that pay well are seen as profitable – that is, successful and therefore more likely to offer long term prospects. Such organisations are also seen as putting a proper value on their employees' contribution.

Applicants do, however, look at the total job package – that is, what they will have to do, the effort required, the hours including starting and finishing times, the physical working conditions and the convenience of travelling to and from work. Applicants will also assess what they will get in return, the amount and security of income, prospects of better pay and/or status, fringe benefits and less tangible things such as whether or not they believe there will be compatible working colleagues. The presence or absence of some of these factors will determine the extent to which the employer might need to add extra to the going rate to attract applicants.

Retaining employees is also a function of the right level of pay but, as many an employer has found to his cost, good pay by itself will not necessarily hold people to a company. Just as applicants look for a number of things in a job, so do existing employees. The priority which they put on various conditions such as pay, security, status and fringe benefits will differ not only from one person to another but also with the same person at different times and in different circumstances. For example, overtime is always more in demand prior to Christmas or vacation times when employees have extra expenses to meet. Young employees who are about to marry or are newly-wed and setting up home will normally put money high on their list of priorities, and be prepared to work longer hours or take on extra responsibilities to maximise their earnings. This may continue over the period when they are providing for a family. At some stage, however, they will probably start to balance extra earnings against the desire to spend more time with their family. Similarly, other needs employees share, for status and security for example, will change in relative importance at different times and in different situations. Those executives involved in recruiting young employees including graduates will be well aware of the importance most of them place on what has come to be called 'quality of life'.

Clearly then, although pay is an important factor in recruiting and retaining employees, unless a company's policies recognise people's other needs it might find it is having to compensate with higher pay than would otherwise be necessary.

Motivating employees to join and stay with an organisation is in most circumstances easier that motivating each of them to use their efforts and abilities to the full to meet its objectives. It has been said that all employee relations problems arise over one side or the other of the wage/effort equation. Over how much 'wage' people get in relation to others within or without the company, and the factors which affect it such as overtime, shift and job allocation, piece-work and bonus systems, job grading and promotion, or over how much 'effort' they are required to expend to meet the employer's requirements, including such factors as time spent on and off the job and at work, skill flexibility and management's methods of maximising effort (e.g. work study and discipline). If this assertion is true, and all the evidence says it is as true as such short general statements can be, then clearly the method by which people are paid, i.e. the system which determines their total earnings particularly in relation to others, is as important as how much they are paid.

Most managers and trade union officials know from experience that establishing and maintaining internal pay relativities is at least as difficult as establishing a level which is seen as competitive with other organisations. They will also know that unless a pay structure is regarded as fair and providing some consistency of earnings it will quickly lead to feelings of injustice and to conflict. In such circumstances money is acting as a demotivator and the organisation's pay policy is not meeting one of its primary objectives. This can occur, as was frequently seen in the past in the print, vehicle, docks and shipbuilding industries, irrespective of the level of earnings workers are receiving.

If such problems are to be avoided then the employer must aim to construct a pattern of differentials which reflects the views of the majority of employees. Using some technique to measure the relative worth of each job such as job evaluation is not necessarily the answer. Some apparently sophisticated job evaluation schemes which ignore employee or union views or traditional job hierarchies, produce results which although supported by sound rationale, still create conflict and feelings of injustice.

Because changing a pay structure, which is a euphemism for changing the pattern of differentials, is so fraught with risks it should only be embarked on by managements convinced that the problems it will resolve are worth the risk of the problems the change may create. The experience of many companies has led to the saying among industrial relations specialists that 'the best wage structure is the one you have'. The risks to established patterns of differentials must be evaluated by anyone considering financial incentives, because while normally such schemes do not change basic hourly rates or weekly or monthly salaries, they will alter earnings. The benefits achieved through financial incentives can be lost overnight through dissatisfaction or conflict.

1.03 Indirect financial incentives

The term 'financial incentive scheme' is most frequently used to describe the method of payment where part of earnings is directly linked to some performance factor, such as achievement of production, delivery or sales target. Many pay structures, however, have elements which can be termed indirect incentives. For example, annual salary reviews, if they depend on management discretion and do not always result in an automatic standard increase, provide an incentive for employees to maintain or improve standards or performance. Pay increases linked to service are an incentive for employees to stay with that employer. Age scales, often used with younger workers, have the same effect. Extra pay for qualifications, such as the practice in the engineering industry of paying draughtsmen with HNC more than those without, provide an incentive to improve vocational knowledge and skills. With young trainees the age and qualification increments can be linked so that the trainee only moves up through the age pay scale, or beyond a certain point, if he has passed the appropriate examination stages.

Merit schemes, once popular with many large employers, still have their management supporters. Their advantage is that they enable the employer to reward particular attributes which he determines as desirable and thereby discriminate between workers, creating an incentive for them to meet his standards. It also introduces an element of flexibility into the pay structure which might be particularly valuable in attracting and keeping skills which are in short supply. Disadvantages stem from these apparent advantages in that unless objective criteria are used as the basis for merit awards, employees will disagree with the validity of management judgements and the awards will become a bone of contention. Sometimes such criticisms will be justified, as some supervisors and managers are prone to letting their emotions influence their decisions and forming opinions about employees based on particular incidents rather than a balanced evaluation of their total contribution over a lengthy period. Industrial Tribunals see regular examples of this when hearing wrongful dismissal claims.

Trade unions dislike merit schemes on both philosophical and practical grounds. They embrace the philosophy that workers are equal and should be paid the same rate for the same job, and refuse to accept that management has the right, or ability, to judge one man's worth over another's. They also know that differences in pay for the same work, unless they can be satisfactorily explained to the employees concerned, create divisions and tensions. Conversely, some managers believe that an element of competition between employees is productive but whether or not it is will depend on the circumstances, not least on whether or not productivity hinges on individual or team effort.

Where the workforce is effectively unionised and a union or unions have collective bargaining rights, special consideration should be given to the cost advantages of any merit scheme. Unless the scheme has significant employee acceptance the unions are likely to maintain pressure to dilute the qualifications, particularly the subjective criteria, and to get it abandoned. Their usual tactics are to get as many employees as possible receiving the merit payments and then press for these to be consolidated into the base wage or salary. This potential risk to labour costs has to be balanced against the advantages management perceives in merit schemes.

When planning a merit payment policy careful consideration also needs to be given to the qualities the employer wants to encourage, bearing in mind the need for measurable criteria whenever possible. Lateness and absence are obviously measurable. Quantity of work may be relatively easy to measure. Quality is easy to measure in some jobs, for example where the employees are making something to predetermined standards or where their performance can be gauged by the number of customer complaints. Where the individual's contribution is obscured by others' efforts, quality is more difficult to assess. In such circumstances management may decide on more subjective standards but in doing so run the risks referred to above.

Willingness to be mobile and accept other work assignments in different departments or on different shifts or overtime is measurable, providing proper records are maintained, and this also could become one of the qualifications for a merit award.

In the case of salaried or more senior staff where a system of annual appraisal is operated, merit can be linked with the achievement of objectives set the previous year. To be successful the objectives should be targets which are within the power of the individual to achieve, and discussed and agreed between him and his immediate superior at the time they are set. This approach also has the advantage of making the performance appraisal system more open and more credible, and encouraging the face-to-face assessment discussion between 'supervisor' and subordinate which so many managers avoid.

If a merit scheme is to act as a motivator and not a demotivator then the criteria for earning merit awards must be known, understood and acceptable to the majority of those affected. It follows, therefore, that communicating the objectives of the scheme and how it will operate is important to its success. Some of the methods described subsequently in the chapter on introducing financial incentives can be used for this purpose.

1.04 Defining the problem

One of the less frequently quoted laws ascribed to that ubiquitous sage Murphy is: 'Whatever you want to do, you have to do something else first'. In the case of management decision-making, the 'something else' is to define the problem, analyse it and evaluate the alternatives. Because of the inherent risks in changing pay structures, as thorough a problem analysis as possible is essential before deciding to introduce a financial incentive scheme.

It is, unfortunately, still too common in British industry for quite significant decisions on personnel policy matters to be made on little more than management hunches or generalised beliefs about their workforce. Executives who insist, quite rightly, on detailed costings, trial runs and laboratory test results before introducing a new machine or material into a process, will make decisions affecting employees, which could in cost terms be far more significant, based on opinions and anecdotal evidence and the flimsiest of data. When collecting and collating information about the problem, which might involve financial incentives as part of the solution, the question has to be constantly asked: 'Is this a fact or an assumption?'. Only by doing that and seeking hard supportive evidence each time will the real problems be uncovered and understood.

The starting point for such questions will be the current assumptions management has made about its problem, assumptions which have led to the consideration of financial incentives. But, first, a word of caution. A survey, carried out by the Department of Employment, of companies that had changed their wage structures showed that frequently the change was made to resolve problems whose roots lay elsewhere – in other words, problems that could not be resolved with a new pay structure. This tendency to seek solutions to other problems by changing pay systems may be due to a carry-over of management thinking from the days when all the faults of British industry were ascribed to the workers or the unions, or a simplistic belief that all problems respond to having money thrown at them.

Insisting on validated data about the perceived problem will have one other important benefit in addition to the obvious one of making sure that the real issues are known and understood. It will quickly show whether the information is available or, alternatively, whether systems to produce the information necessary to create and control a financial incentive scheme can be speedily and economically set up. Incentive schemes, like tax collections, need to show a good return over and above the cost of administration.

There are various ways the task of problem analysis can be tackled, and the method selected will largely depend on resources. Providing they are given tight terms of reference, consultants are ideal for this sort of study but can prove expensive. They are probably not as expensive, however, as a wrong decision about an incentive scheme! An internal task force which should preferably include a work study engineer or organisation and methods specialist and a cost analyst, or people trained in these techniques, could prove as effective as, but lack the objectivity of, consultants. If internal resources are used, then they need to have the authority and support of the board in their task and given the time and other facilities needed. To avoid suspicion and their efforts being misconstrued, wherever possible all employees should be told who the task force are and what they are doing. Part of the process they use for gathering information should include speaking to all, or representatives of all, levels of management and supervision and the various functions in the company. It should not be assumed, for example, that the sales employees have no contribution to make to the study of what appears to be a production problem, or that production supervision staff do not have useful views about what is believed to be a marketing difficulty. Frequently the employees closest to the product or the customer are those at the bottom of the hierarchy, but seldom take part in the discussion of problems. Some means of involving these people will pay dividends when trying to understand the problem and develop solutions.

We are all at some time or another guilty of a blinkered approach to problems, and it is useful to step back and start from basics. This can certainly be a productive approach when considering the appropriateness of financial incentives. Management's basic task is to organise the supply and utilisation of human resources, materials and facilities in a cost-effective way. As far as the human element is involved, this means getting the right numbers and mixture of skills, establishing the appropriate organisation structure, ensuring everyone knows what they have to do and has the tools, materials, facilities, training and motivation to do it. Clearly where the desired results are not being achieved it can be due to a number of factors, all of which are the responsibility of management.

Inadequate selection methods, either for external recruits or internal promotions, will lead to the wrong people in the wrong jobs. Insufficient attention to training results in employees at all levels, including supervision and management, having inadequate skills. Poor communication results in people not really understanding what is required of them. A faulty organisation structure can lead to duplication of effort or, more frequently, to tasks not being done because of confusion over lines of responsibility. The list is endless, but all or any of these things can quickly result in lack of clear direction of the most valuable resources of an organisation, its people. If this is the problem it may be shown up more clearly if incentive payments are introduced, but it is doubtful if the payments system by itself will resolve it.

Studies into the claimed successes of financial incentive schemes have shown that often it is the indirect effects which have generated the most benefit. Examples, include cases where employees would not accept work study until it was linked with payment by results, and where the major advantages to management came from being able to measure for the first time how much labour was really needed. In other cases, continuity of production was achieved because workers, whose earnings were now affected by them, identified the bottlenecks, Clearly, therefore, incentive payment schemes can draw attention to problems which management should be identifying and tackling. This emphasises the importance of a thorough and objective analysis of an organisation's problems before deciding on the introduction of financial incentives.

The answer to the question 'Why do we need an incentive payment scheme?' should ideally be 'We believe we have a workforce which is well organised and well trained, led and supervised by people who are themselves well trained both technically and in man management. We have adequate and on-going methods for communicating with and involving all employees so they feel part of the organisation and understand its problems and objectives. We have personnel policies which generate loyalty and commitment because they make employees feel that we are concerned about them, and believe that their efforts will result in their improved security and opportunities to advance their status and conditions. We now think that we can further improve the company's performance by linking pay with results and giving employees a more direct financial link between their contribution to the organisation and their income.' That is an ideal answer but a close examination of how far that statement is true in any situation, plus an evaluation of how well the basic tasks of 'organising the supply and utilisation of human resources' referred to above are being carried out will give a good starting point to any study.

1.05 Who needs motivating?

A thorough and objective study of the organisation's problems should not only show whether the solution, in full or part, lies in financial incentives but also who those incentives should be aimed at. Unless it has been thorough and objective, internal vested interests or just plain woolly thinking could lead to a lot of money being spent in the wrong direction. Paying production bonuses to direct workers whose output is governed by the speed of the machine maintenance service they receive, or paying sales bonuses to representatives whose real problem is poor product design, faulty pricing policy or inadequate market research, is clearly not a good commercial proposition: i.e. it will not give an adequate return on the investment. The most common mistake made when introducing incentive schemes is to assume that the key to raising productivity is motivating the bottom rung, the clerical or manual workers, when the problem is one of management.

Correctly identifying the target group is a necessary step before deciding on the type of incentive scheme to consider. The study will show whether the need is to motivate one or more groups or the whole workforce in a company or other organisation. This will be the primary consideration in deciding on the type of scheme to adopt.

Chapter 2

The Arguments For And Against Financial Incentives

2.01 The philosophical arguments

The fact that in some industries the proportion of people on payment by results is approximately 50 per cent, and successful companies exist that use incentive systems and equally successful ones that do not, make it obvious that there are valid arguments both for and against such methods of payment. These arguments can be divided into the philosophical and the practical.

The philosophical arguments explained at length in many textbooks, and usually linked with an account of the development of management thought and the work of pioneers such as Frederick Taylor and Mary Parker Follett, are extensive. The argument most generally heard, however, is that an efficient management with competent supervision should organise and control the flow of work in a way which maintains output and quality standards. These can be constantly improved, the argument continues, by investment in more modern facilities and better methods. Paying wages and salaries and applying other conditions which are competitive will enable the organisation to hire employees of adequate calibre to fulfill these objectives, and the absence of incentives gives a predictability of labour costs and encourages the full exercise of management's skills and responsibility. People being paid to do a job should not be paid extra for working to a proper standard. It is management's job to set the standards and see they are achieved, using whatever techniques are appropriate in the circumstances.

Those who support incentives will say that they do not quarrel with most of that but the best that such managements will achieve is average employee effort; to get more requires some additional motivator and the most powerful motivator is money. If properly applied, incentive schemes can aid predictability of costs, because they will be based on more measurable data on employee performance per unit.

2.02 The practical arguments against incentives

The practical arguments on both sides carry more weight because they are, by and large, more supportable by hard evidence, whereas the philosophical can only be demonstrated in general terms and in the ultimate depends on individual management conviction. The practical arguments against incentives can be summarised as follows.

Financial incentive schemes tend to reward, and therefore put emphasis on the quantitative rather than the qualitative aspects of output and service, and even if quality is built into the reward criteria it is always easier to cut corners on it because it is usually less tangible, i.e. less measurable, than quantity. This is the most widely used argument against incentive schemes, and one that cannot lightly be ignored. Its validity, however, must depend on circumstances, particularly the extent to which quality can be accurately measured and is in the control of the employee. It also raises questions about the position of those responsible for ensuring that quality standards are met: for example, can their independence be maintained if they are part of the scheme? If they ar not to be part of the scheme, what will happen to their differential, assuming one exists, if the direct worker can boost his earnings by higher output? Will people still want to be inspectors if production operators have a higher earnings potential?

This leads into what is probably the next most widely used argument, that financial incentive schemes distort differentials. Where it is a scheme which applies to less than the whole workforce including supervision and management, this will almost certainly be the case. Continuing with the example of a direct labour only incentive scheme, this would, if successful, narrow the differentials between them and indirect workers such as skilled maintenance and toolroom craftsmen and supervisors, and widen their differential over labourers.

The inverse differentials created by payments by results systems in the Midlands engineering industry, which gave semi-skilled production operators higher pay than toolmakers, led to difficulties over many years. It eventually resulted in an agreement in Coventry giving toolmakers the district average earnings of production workers. These lieu bonuses, as they are generally called, can create further anomalies, leading to misunderstanding and conflict about hitherto simple, well understood and accepted pay structures.

Many of the practical arguments against incentive schemes become even more significant where the workforce is unionised, as clearly incentives mean money and a union's primary objective is to raise the earnings of its members. Although some union representatives are openly opposed to such schemes, believing them to be divisive or encouraging unsafe working practices etc., the majority are in favour. This is probably because they recognise they can boost earnings and provide another fruitful area of negotiation.

There are advantages to unions and employees and disadvantages to management in incentive schemes which give scope for regular renegotiation of the terms when, for example, one of the factors such as product or process changes. Where such negotiation takes place at workshop or office level, that is where management's bargaining skills are probably weakest and the risks to costs are evident.

The danger of wage drift, defined as a tendency for earnings to increase considerably faster than wage rates, is an argument used especially by those for whom predictable labour costs are essential for planning purposes. A survey of wages drift carried out some years ago on behalf of the now extinct Prices and Incomes Board, showed it was most prevalent in those industries or sections of industry where payment by results predominated as a system of payment.

Incentive schemes which involve bargaining at workshop level can also create a situation where those doing the bargaining have more influence on earnings than those who negotiate base rates and conditions. This can greatly increase the power of individual shop stewards above that of senior stewards or full-time union officials, and undermine established collective bargaining arrangements. This may or may not be a serious consideration depending on how existing arrangements are viewed, but it has to be recognised that in any case where employee relations are bad an incentive scheme can quickly become another point of conflict.

It was a combination of such problems which led the then British Leyland management to strive for years to replace incentive pay systems with one common structure of measured day work. Only later, when they felt they had their labour relations well under control did they introduce a tightly administered scheme of production bonus payments. It is indeed arguable whether such a scheme could have been introduced in circumstances other than those which prevailed following Sir Michael Edwardes' reforms.

Where an organisation's workforce is unionised, any incentive scheme will have to be negotiated and the unions will look for safeguards for their members. Except in the very simplest scheme there will be scope for differences of interpretation, giving the unions an on-going role. Those involved in the negotiations will become the authorities referred to for judgements when differences arise. A common example is in schemes based on output which define the effect on payments when output increases as a result of capital investment. If it results in changes for employees in what they do or how the work is organised then the unions will be looking for, at the minimum, protection of bonus earnings. It might appear at first sight that providing for such contingencies is a simple matter of agreement drafting, but it can prove complicated in practice. Careful thought given to such matters in the early planning stages of an incentive scheme can save a lot of trouble later on. Incentive payments which create resistance to change and inhibit investment in new equipment and processes can be self-defeating.

Other practical difficulties which can result from payments linked to individual output are reduced labour mobility as employees refuse to move from jobs where they can maximise earnings, and – in any scheme – employee dissatisfaction because of fluctuating earnings. Just as managements like to plan on a stable and predictable cost base so do employees like to plan for domestic expenses, holidays etc., on predictable earnings.

This desire to stabilise earnings is a contributory factor in employees agreeing among themselves, or deciding as individuals to 'cap' their output at a certain level when the facility exists to produce more and earn more. This is a not uncommon situation in machine shops on individual piece-work, and may or may not be influenced by the union.

Where earnings do fluctuate widely, or where there is a significant difference between average earnings and basic pay, pressure will probably be applied to management for an agreement giving guaranteed minimum bonus (sometimes termed fall-back pay). There will also be a demand for holiday pay, sick pay and pensions to be linked to this guaranteed level. Most organisations faced with these pressures make some concessions, usually in the area of holiday pay. Sometimes employers can gain some advantage from such arrangements, for example, if a peak demand for a product is during April, May and June; holiday pay for holidays taken in July based on average earnings in the previous three months can stimulate output during the main selling period. The management saying about turning problems into opportunities is equally applicable to employee relations situations.

Although the risks to quality and safety caused by workers cutting corners to earn more bonus are well recognised, the risks to equipment are not always so obvious. No one knows as much about an operation as the man doing it. He will quickly learn how to adapt a machine or system for his own ends – more pay. Machines run at the wrong speeds, or given the quick fix instead of the proper but more time-consuming repairs, are possibilities managers have to be alert to if expensive equipment is not to have a shortened life span, or tool costs are not to go through the roof.

All financial incentive schemes have a limited life at the end of which they have to be abandoned or modified to meet changed conditions. Opponents of incentives argue that inevitably some element of the bonus or piece-rate will be built into the new rate as part of the cost of change, and thus raises the new pay to a higher level than it would otherwise have been. Experience suggests they are right, and, of course, when this stage is reached it is often because the scheme is no longer cost-effective as a motivator, i.e. the employee is already getting money for little or no extra effort.

2.03 The practical arguments for incentives

Writers on management, including those who are stronger on theory than practice, will accept that money is a motivator, and this has to be top of the list of arguments for using it. Put simplistically, the manager's job is to get people to do things. The good manager understands that there is a whole range of techniques to be used in different circumstances, and can assess which should be used, where, and when, and is capable of successfully using them. No one technique is suitable in all situations. A participative or authoritarian management style, consultation, communication, direction, all have their place in the manager's tool-box, and like a good craftsman he needs to know which tool or tools to reach for. Some, like communication, will stay in use all the time; others will be used more selectively.

Supporters of financial incentives argue that because employees want to increase their earnings they will co-operate with efforts to achieve higher production if it also means more money. They will, for example, accept work measurement which they would otherwise reject, believing it to be in the employer's interest rather than theirs. The arguments go beyond that. If more pay depends on more output, they and their representatives will take an active part in identifying things which restrict output. The tool changes, material shortages or mechanical or system failures which once meant a welcome break from work routine become irksome restrictions on earnings, to be eliminated or kept as short as possible – assuming that the scheme has been properly designed.

Such employee participation can also result in improvements in ways which were not foreseen when the incentives were introduced. Employees may improve working methods and procedures, and not only their own. They may spot the weaknesses in the material control functions which are affecting their efforts. Their criticism of maintenance delays may highlight the tool or parts shortages which extend machine downtime. Deficiences in purchased materials which affect the ability to produce quality, and, therefore, bonus earnings, may point to faulty purchasing procedures or inadequate attention to supplier quality. Workers' representatives will ask questions showing up weaknesses which vested interests, or just complacency in management areas, may not readily expose.

The amount of time which employees spend actually working will also probably increase where financial incentives are used. People tend to adopt a standard of living which matches their earnings, and periods off work due to sickness, for example, become more of a hardship where incentive pay creates a big gap between earnings at work and income off work. No responsible employer wants people at work who are unfit, but most studies of sickness absence show periods of such absence are often extended more than necessary.

Casual absence of the one- or two-day kind, which in some organisations is more difficult to contend with, can also be reduced for the same reason – a day's absence where incentive pay is lost costs an employee more than a day lost at base pay. While not every employee will be prepared to sacrifice 'leisure' for money, this assertion is valid as a generalisation about human behaviour.

The right type of incentives, the supporters will argue, can go even beyond this and create an interest in and identification with the organisation's objectives and problems, and do this more successfully than employee participation programmes which invite employees' contribution without giving any share in the results except promises of greater job security.

Claims that incentive schemes give a better base for manpower budgeting are only valid if incentives are necessary to buy co-operation with proper work measurement, and some strong supporters of incentives have no experience of work measurement except as part of an incentive pay policy. Clearly, if designed to do so, incentives can lead to a more efficient use of labour, for example, as an aid in breaking down demarcations and even as a means of buying co-operation in the reduction of headcount, thus reducing unit labour costs.

It needs to be stressed that with or without incentives, work measurement is an important management tool. Whether applied in the factory, shop or office, however, it needs to be used by people trained in the technique. Properly applied work measurement, which is essential in individual incentive schemes, also ensures a fair distribution of work, enables objective targets to be set, helps in identifying blockages, provides a basis for costing and manpower budgeting, and provides a means of measuring the results of changes in layout, mechanisation, etc.

2.04 The role of the supervisor

The role of the supervisor is often overlooked when companies plan incentive schemes. Without incentives the supervisor uses a range of techniques to maximise the efforts of those under him. It is a difficult job, especially in circumstances where alternative work for employees is available in the area, and the trade union has rights of representation at the workplace. Supervisors are often inadequately trained for their job, and often possess only the same skills and education level as their subordinates. Indeed some managements would argue that pound for pound, money spent on supervisor training is in the longer term a more productive investment than money spent on any other way of motivating employees.

When incentive payments are introduced for the first time, the supervisor's role changes, perhaps significantly. Normally he will have to devote less time to ensuring that the work effort is maintained and more time to planning a constant work flow, and promptly dealing with issues raised by employees which they claim are interrupting effort and earnings. In other words, instead of pressurising employees to maintain constant effort he could find employees pressurising him to tackle shortages, breakdowns etc. Where individual incentives operate he might also find it more difficult to allocate tasks or, even worse, find himself acting as a rate-fixer or constantly arguing about the incentive pay formula.

The most favourable effect on the supervisor's role occurs when the scheme in use reduces the need for him to spend as much time on man management, and allows him to devote more effort to planning, method improvement etc. Whatever the effect, however, it needs to be recognised that the supervisor's role will change, and that change will call for a different balance of supervisory skills. Depending on the extent and nature of the change, management will need to consider additional training and perhaps, even seek different types of people to fill the job in the future. The reverse situation, eliminating incentives and using measured day work for example, poses similar problems for supervision and calls for similar actions from management.

The effect of incentive schemes on differentials has already been referred to, and nothing will demotivate loyal supervisors faster than a scheme which results in those they supervise earning as much or more than they do. A prudent management will foresee this and either adjust the supervisor's pay accordingly or introduce improvements in pay, fringes, privileges, status or a combination of these, which will make them feel good about the change. The changes in their role might provide the vehicle to facilitate this in a rational and cost-effective manner.

The risk of just transferring the differential problem to another level in the management ranks emphasises the importance of making changes to the compensation structure as part of a total strategy: a subject dealt with in a later chapter.

Chapter 3

The Essential Ingredients For The Successful Use Of Financial Incentives

3.01 Defining success

Most organisations measure success in terms of achievement of profit or budget objectives. That obvious generalisation, however, encompasses a whole collection of subsidiary objectives which organisations have, some clearly related to profit and costs, others less directly so. Optimum utilisation of installed capacity and human resources is directly related to profitability. A company's image in the community, however, in the short term and in most circumstances, will not affect its profits. In the longer term, however, it may affect its ability to recruit the type of skills it needs to continue in business or affect the demand for its product. Improving or maintaining the organisation's image, therefore, would be seen by most directors as an important objective.

Financial incentive schemes, therefore, need not be viewed only in terms of increasing employee effort to make the organisation immediately more profitable, but also considered as a possible means of meeting a whole range of primary and subsidiary objectives. The key role of the board, or senior executive responsible for remuneration, is to define the objective to be met and also, if possible, at that same stage define what would be accepted as proof of success. If the problem is low sales penetration, success would obviously be higher penetration; if it is absenteeism success would be reduced absence; if it is excessive scrap success would be an acceptable level of scrap; if it is delays in deliveries, processing invoices or handling customers' complaints success would be less delays. In each case the problem must be measurable, and the factors contributing to it must also be measurable. If they are not then it will be difficult to evaluate accurately the effects of changing one factor, the pay of the people involved, and impossible to tell whether the incentive is cost-effective.

As the board of a company has the right to use financial resources in what it judges to be the corporate interest, it could decide to introduce an incentive scheme for what might be termed public relations reasons. Because a company's image with the public at large partly depends on on how it is seen to treat its employees, it may decide to introduce profit sharing or employee share ownership, for example, without evidence that this would improve the workforce contribution to profit over and above the cost of the scheme but in the hope that it will improve the public's perception of the company in a way which produces indirect advantages. Such considerations are, however, outside the scope of this book, as we are concerned here only with methods of using incentives in a cost-effective way to influence employees' performance.

3.02 The essential ingredients

Having systematically defined the problem and objective – an essential first requirement for success in anything management does – the next step is to establish whether the solution, wholly or in part, lies in the hands of employees and if so which employees. In other words, where does the responsibility for improved performance lie? Who can change the situation from what it is to what it should be? Here, as at other stages, the corporate philosophy may influence decisions. Some organisations take the view that as it is management's responsibility to get results, it is their failure if the necessary results are not being achieved. This will not preclude the use of incentives but their use in these circumstances is more likely to follow an evaluation of whether that is the correct technique for the organisation to use in that situation. In organisations that are defensive about their management's abilities and, thereby, less objective, there will be a greater willingness to accept uncritically that the fault lies at the bottom rungs. Some organisations see employees as just a necessary cost like office space or machines; others view them as a valuable resource which requires investment.

Whatever thought process leads to the conclusion that financial incentives will help, getting the right target group is essential if money is to be spent productively – that is, where it will produce the best return. If the problem has been the subject of a systematic and objective study as described in Chapter 1, the results will have indicated the course of action that needs pursuing. The experience of most readers will tell them that more than one action will probably be needed, as few problems have simple answers and such studies often highlight deficiencies in organisation, skill, training, or facilities as well as weaknesses in areas like forecasting and design.

Two studies in the 1980s of productivity, one in toolmaking and the other in metal manufacturing companies in Britain and West Germany, showed that lack of technical training and education at all levels in the British companies was one of the most significant factors contributing to their lower productivity. Differences in skill and knowledge standards at the manual worker level were not, however, as significant as the lack of technical training in supervision and management. The effects of this percolated through to the quality of management decisions, including those on the purchase and utilisation of equipment. This illustrates the dangers of jumping to conclusions about causes.

Although the problem analysis may indicate a specific target area, that does not preclude the use of an incentive scheme which covers all employees. Thought needs to be given, however, to the cost-effectiveness of paying all employees to resolve a problem, the solution to which lies with a few. There is, however, a vast difference between deciding to do something after the proper analysis and knowing all the weaknesses and pitfalls and, what is unfortunately still too common, making decisions based on inadequate research and treating assumptions as facts.

If the aim is to raise the general level of performance, then the problem analysis and definition of objective must be at the corporate level where the necesssary qualifications can be added. For example, success may require investment in new products. This cannot be determined by employees so objectives set – if they are to be realistic, i.e. achievable – would have to be limited to what can be done with existing products until the investment is made and bears fruit. The most sophisticated or costly incentive schemes cannot motivate employees to do what is not within their power. Employees must have the means of improving their own performance. Another essential ingredient, therefore, is that the employees must have the ability to do whatever it is the incentive is being paid for. It is a waste of money to give financial incentives to clerks if what is needed is a new computer program, or to direct production workers when the key is better tooling. Because incentive pay has a nasty habit of eventually becoming part of base remuneration, such mistakes can have disastrous long-term effects on wage and salary costs.

Incentive payments also appear to work best where the product and process are not subject to constant change, and where production schedules are not subject to wide fluctuations. Where these factors do exist there is a high risk that disagreements will occur over the validity of the incentive criteria in the different circumstances, and dissatisfaction with fluctuations in earning ability.

If employees are to be motivated to change their behaviour in a way which improves their performance they must be able to recognise a link between what they do and what they get in return. In other words, cause and effect need to be easily demonstrable. The most effective incentives are the simplest ones. Such an example is where an employee, who has total control of his output and previously produced fifty pieces of acceptable quality in a set period of time, knows he will earn twice as much if he produces a hundred in the same time. He can see a clear relationship between his effort and his wage packet. Anything which obscures that relationship detracts from the motivational value of the incentive pay. Unfortunately, the circumstances which make such simple schemes practical are rare. Normally it is necessary to devise a formula which provides for factors outside the employees' and employer's control, such as lack of material or orders or changes to product or process.

As well as being able to understand the way incentive pay is earned, employees must believe it is fair. A scheme which gives the employer 80 per cent of the gains in output, and employees 20 per cent, for example, would not be seen as just and is more likely to lead to resentment than increased effort. It also follows that there has to be at minimum the type of relationship where employees trust the management to administer the payments scheme honestly. This generally means a scheme where the method of calculation is known and is open for inspection by employees or their representatives.

To be seen as fair, and if it is to act as a motivator, then the scheme must ensure that extra pay is only earned for effort above the normal standard. If any employees are able to get the additional pay for no change in performance, the scheme will be seen as unjust, lose credibility and, in the process, its motivational effect. This again illustrates the importance of measurable criteria both to establish the standard and to gauge effort above standard.

To overcome the inherent risk of employees producing quantity at the expense of quality to earn extra money, it is essential that management has the means to protect quality standards. In some circumstances this will pose no problem; in others the cost of extra quality checks will need to be set against the gains of extra output. In some situations the first practical check on quality is the customer. Disputes about responsibility for poor quality in those circumstances are seldom productive or conclusive, or good for sales.

In summary, the essential ingredients for a successful financial incentive scheme are a situation which can be changed by a change in employee performance, and where the employees have control over their own output, clear and measurable performance objectives, identifying the employees who can achieve them, a scheme which is seen as fair to both management and employees, where the link between increased effort and reward is easily understood and recognised, where extra pay only comes from extra effort, where both existing standards and performance above standard are measurable, and where management has the means to protect quality.

3.03 Evaluating the pros and cons in different situations

The executive is fortunate who can start off in a green field situation and decide what pay structure to adopt. More often he is considering introducing incentives into an established organisation with its own history, traditions and attitudes about pay. It might be that payment by results is the norm, or conversely the exception, for that type of business.

In weighing up the advantages and disadvantages of using incentives, a whole range of considerations will have to be examined such as costs, negotiability, controllability of costs and quality, management and supervisory capability, and the impact on differentials and employee relations. These considerations will apply even if it is decided to introduce incentives as a stop-gap while longer term measures such as the appointment of new managers, supervisory training or investment in new facilities or products are pursued.

In assessing the costs, judgements will need to be made about likely improvements, what effect these will have at different levels of performance, not forgetting to include the scheme's administration cost. If no clear margin of gain is likely, this should call for a re-think. In a unionised environment, where the scheme will have to be negotiated, adjustments to the estimates will also have to be made for the difference between the formula management wants and what the unions are likely to accept.

The costs of administering incentive payments will also differ from organisation to organisation, depending on the extent to which regular returns on output and quality or other performance measurements are already produced. Even where such information is available it will most likely have to be supplemented to establish the controls needed. When people's pay depends on it, performance data has to be both accurate and 'fiddle-proof'. The sensible manager will set up a trial system to provide this information, both to test its reliability and to estimate the costs involved before finalising his plans.

Where employee relations are good and the facility exists to elicit employees' views, management should be able to get some prior appreciation of how incentives would be accepted if a selective incentive scheme is being considered, i.e. one that would not apply to the whole workforce, then upsetting the established pattern of differentials is a problem which employees will quickly recognise. Where employee relations are bad the risks of tampering with the pay structure would not be worth taking unless all the other factors and the estimated gains were highly favourable.

The capability of management, and particularly supervision, to cope with the changes created by incentives must be assessed. Being supportive of the proposal does not necessarily mean they are able to accommodate the change, especially if the type of scheme envisaged will give them a more demanding role.

Even a successful incentive plan can create problems which are best handled if considered in advance. Apart from the need to be able to sell additional products or services which result from improved performance, such improvements might put an extra load on maintenance, transport, accounts or other services, or show up shortages in storage space or other facilities. Although these are the type of problems most organisations would welcome, in some circumstances the costs of expanding support services and facilities might be prohibitive.

Evaluating your own situation to determine whether financial incentives have a role is therefore largely a question of first making sure you have all the information and feeling confident that you know the root cause of the problem. Second, seeing that the essential ingredients for successfully using incentives are present, and last but not least, making sure you have thought through all the alternative courses of action.

3.04 Considering alternatives

It is, of course, impossible to describe every combination of circumstances in which financial incentives might be thought of as a solution, or to describe steps which could be used as alternatives, but the following illustrate the wide range of measures available in most situations.

Improving management morale

Because the success of any organisation depends to a large degree on the enthusiasm and commitment of the management team, low management morale is a serious problem which can be the cause, or a symptom, of other problems. Before leaping to the conclusion that the answer lies in a management bonus plan or some other financial incentive, it is worth reflecting on some of the other techniques to rebuild morale.

Problems often arise in management ranks because their loyalty and commitment is taken for granted, and it is wrongly assumed that managers do not have the aims, fears and concerns of other employees. Managers, just like office, shop, farm or factory workers, need praise, encouragement, recognition for efforts as well as salary; in other words they need to know how they stand. In addition, if they are to feel and act as managers they need *information* – information which enables them to understand corporate plans, policies and objectives so they can play their part effectively and carry their subordinates with them. One of the quickest ways to demoralise a management team and produce insecurity is to pass on decisions without explanations, and force it to rely on rumour or the media to find out what is happening.

Faced with a management morale problem the board might consider ways of building up confidence and commitment, and a team approach to the corporate goals. A well tried way of doing this is the management conference. To be successful this needs to be well prepared. The senior executives responsible need to define the objectives of the conference and prepare the programme. Only such jobs as booking the venue, arranging transport and catering should be delegated, and only then with clear terms of reference regarding standards and costs.

The objectives will be to build an enthusiastic management team with knowledge and understanding of the organisation's goals, problems, strategies, plans and policies, and to get their commitment to these. To achieve this the board members or senior executives concerned will need to demonstrate a thorough understanding of the organisation, its products and markets, a clear grasp of the issues facing the organisation, and a credible plan for the future. Only if they can do this will they create confidence in the leadership; a vital factor in raising and maintaining the morale of subordinates.

Although of necessity, at the first of such conferences much of the time will be spent giving information to the audience, some time in the programme should be allocated when everyone can contribute in some way. There are various techniques for achieving this which produce better results than just asking for questions from the platform. Many people, including competent managers, are reticent about standing up in a large gathering. Those that will do so may only do it to be noticed and might not be those who could make the best contribution.

One way of achieving broader participation is to divide managers into mixed seminar groups to address particular issues. They might, for example, be asked to suggest ways of improving communications in the organisation. Working as a group with an elected spokesman enables contentious points to be raised with a degree of anonymity. Obviously such techniques are more suitable with the larger conference, but a small company with a closely knit team of managers might profitably consider extending the conference to embrace others with a contribution to make, such as representatives in the field who do not normally come together with 'head office'. Clearly there are an infinite number of variations on the theme, but if well handled, managers should go away feeling they have been treated as responsible individuals with an important part to play in achieving the corporate objectives. Their morale will have been raised. This enthusiasm will soon wane, however, if the conference is the only evidence of change, and on return to their offices they feel isolated and ill-informed. Such conferences should, therefore, if they are to have maximum impact, be used as a plank on which to build closer relationships and structures for keeping management in the picture. Nearly all organisations could benefit from a communications policy based on the simple rule that everyone should know as much as is practical about what is going on, and in most circumstances the only limitations need be those required for commercial secrecy, such as information about new products which would be of advantage to competitors.

A philosophy of only telling employees what they need to know to do their job does not usually prove productive with managers or any other employees.

Tackling management or supervisory morale problems by creating status symbols to make them feel recognised is an alternative that needs to be approached with some caution. Providing foremen with smart overall coats with the corporate logo inscribed, or separate canteen and toilet facilities can play a part in improving their morale, but introducing conditions which separate out groups or individuals can create divisions when the corporate need might be to weld all employees into one team. It is, however, easy to exaggerate such effects, and judgements can only be made in the knowledge of all the circumstances. Britain is a country where signs of status have always existed and where, for the most part, they are accepted, but there is a trend towards breaking down some traditional barriers such as that between manual and office worker. If the organisation anticipates joining this movement it will hesitate before creating more distinctions, and reward the contribution of managers in other ways.

A performance appraisal system, whether linked to management development and compensation plans or not, can play a part in improving morale by providing an opportunity for the counselling of managers, and for discussing their performance and future. If treated seriously by all concerned, performance counselling interviews will provide early warning of management problems while at the same time providing a mechanism for building confidence and enthusiasm.

Maintenance workers

The not uncommon problem of slow and costly maintenance provides another example where alternative actions might be considered. It is possible to design a financial incentive scheme specially for maintenance workers based on average repair times with rewards for work completed faster, but before seizing at such solutions there are a number of other actions worth considering.

Many maintenance departments have grown up on the 'fix it when it breaks' philosophy. Unfortunately, when it does break this can lead to delays in production, service or delivery, and the loss of customer goodwill, if not customers themselves. Substituting a system of planned maintenance to reduce these risks requires proper records of the age of equipment and key components, frequency of and time between breakdowns etc., so that preventive maintenance schedules can be drawn up and disruptive breakdowns minimised. It might also have the effect of reducing the inventory of spares held.

The attitude of the chief maintenance engineer or supervisor could be a critical factor. Most maintenance supervisors are promoted from the ranks of craftsmen with no training in management or knowledge of how other organisations run their maintenance function. This situation may be resolved by training, either a specially designed series of lectures at a local technical college, or visits to other organisations to see their maintenance systems. This latter is likely to have more impact than classroom training, and might be arranged through the employers' federation, a body such as the Industrial Society or the British Institute of Management, or by personally contacting other organisations and seeking their co-operation. The solution to the poor maintenance problem, however, might be simply a question of investing in better tools and equipment and materials, or ensuring that the production managers free up their facilities more often for routine adjustments, lubrication, etc. Whatever the cause it will probably pay to adopt a participative approach. Explaining the problem and its effects on the business to all the maintenance personnel and inviting their ideas could pay dividends. Skilled maintenance men are generally intelligent and interested enough to make a positive contribution to any discussion if the scene has been set correctly. This involvement in defining the problem can be extended to the development of the solutions, and will help to get them accepted.

Incentives for salesmen

Although selling on commission is one of the most common uses of financial incentives, many successful companies do not reward their salesmen this way. The job of a sales representative, which usually carries with it a company car and freedom from close supervision, is sufficiently attractive compared with that of the office, shop or factory workers to make its retention an incentive in itself. In most situations a combination of a competitive salary, training in the organisation's products or services and sales techniques, good supervision, the setting of stretching but achievable targets, and regular morale boosting sales conferences encouraging competition between salesmen, can produce the desired results without the cost of financial incentives.

Reducing absenteeism

Attendance bonuses to reduce absenteeism, which have been used for a long time in the mining industry, are described in the next chapter. These often cause controversy among managers, some of whom feel strongly that it is just paying employees for what they should do anyway. Because of the pitfalls of such bonus schemes, any management faced with a serious absenteeism problem should first consider its whole process of recording and handling absence.

Like most problems, absenteeism cannot be resolved until it is understood. Casual daily absence calls for different action than periods of sickness absence. Absence confined to particular departments, shifts or occupations, will need to be tackled differently from absence across the whole workforce. The key to understanding the problem is a method of recording which not only shows the position on any one day, but enables histories and trends to be easily recognised. As every manager knows, a pattern of Monday and Friday absence, and days immediately before and after holidays is a reasonable, but not infallible, guide to malingering. Regular lateness and absence on Mondays or following pay days can sometimes indicate an employee who drinks too much. Organisations which work different shift patterns may need to design records which highlight absence linked to rest days rather than week-ends.

Armed with sufficient information to tackle the problem a prudent management will ensure that absenteeism is dealt with in a systematic way. Sickness absence supported by medical certificates requires a regular follow-up. Letters or visits to the employee in hospital or at home, or a combination of the two can be used to demonstrate the employer's concern about his employees, to help with any welfare problems the employee may be experiencing, and to encourage a speedy return when he is fit again. In rare cases this process will also identify malingering.

Casual daily absence can often be reduced by insisting that anyone absent is interviewed on his return prior to being allowed to start work. Management's consistency in treating absence as a potential disciplinary offence is important in creating the right attitudes. Slackness by supervisors who might be reluctant to tackle offenders can be a contributory factor in an absence problem.

Where the reasons for absence are unacceptable to management a process of recorded progressive disciplinary action such as verbal warnings, written warnings and suspension (where the contract of employment permits it), will either achieve the objective, i.e. an improvement in the attendance record, or be an essential part of defending management's actions at a Tribunal if the ultimate step of dismissal is taken and then contested by the employee.

If the study of the organisation's problem does suggest that a change in employee behaviour is the key, it does not follow that this is best achieved by introducing an incentive scheme. Money can be used as a motivator to change in other ways – for example, through a process of productivity bargaining or amending the pay structure, enabling plus payments to reward such characteristics as willingness to acquire new skills or move between jobs. These approaches are dealt with in more detail later on.

3.05 The importance of management controls

The basic requirements for effective management control in any organisation are established targets and a regular flow of timely, accurate and relevant information which enables regular comparisons to be made with what is happening and what should be happening to meet those targets, to spot deviations from course and put a correcting hand on the tiller. In some organisations these periodic comparisons are quarterly, six-monthly or even annually, and cover the organisation's overall performance. In others they take place weekly or even daily, with interlocking targets set down to the foreman level. The size and nature of the organisation will partly determine what is needed, but the basic requirements remain the same – targets and information.

Depending on the nature of the products or services produced, the cost of employing people can range from 1 per cent to 99 per cent of total costs. Most organisations fall within the middle range, which means that the personnel cost is a significant factor in determining whether they make a profit or meet their budget objectives. A system of control which embraces recruitment, direct and indirect wages and salaries, overtime, fringe benefits and time on and off the job is, therefore, important. A loosely established and administered incentive scheme can quickly cause runaway personnel costs, and this has contributed to many a company's downfall. If escalating costs in a scheme are to be avoided then there are a number of key requirements, most of which have already been referred to. The most important is to establish a standard which ensures that extra pay is only paid for performance above the level previously and normally obtaining. Without such a standard, pay costs will automatically rise.

The information and controls devised will need to cover quality as well as quantity measurement and, in most circumstances, all the factors which can affect performance such as time on the job, equipment downtime, material availability and scrap.

Although the majority of employees are honest, they will be quick to take advantage of loopholes in a scheme which enables them to boost their earnings for little or no extra effort. An employer who provides such opportunities will be regarded as fair game, and will get little sympathy from employees or unions if his costs go 'through the roof'.

Chapter 4

The Choice Of Schemes Available

4.01 The main types

If anyone contemplating using financial incentives has carried out the steps recommended so far – that is, thoroughly analysed the problem, considered the alternatives and is satisfied that all the essential ingredients for success exist – he will start to look at what is available. Although some slight modifications to them might be needed to fit individual circumstances, there are plenty of well-tried incentive schemes around, and there is no need for any manager to 're-invent the wheel'.

The terms 'piece-work' and 'bonus' are often used loosely to mean different things or to cover any system of payment by results. There are, however, many varied systems of payment by results which can be split into two main categories – individual and group.

Generally speaking, piece-work schemes where the employee is paid a price for each piece or number of pieces produced are individual, although schemes where a small team are paid a price for a piece jointly produced are not unknown. With individual piece-work the method adopted is usually very much the same. The job is work studied and a rate-fixer sets the rate or price for the job. This rate is either accepted or becomes the subject of negotiation between the employee or his representative and the management. Rates for piece-work can either be simply a straight payment of *X* pence per piece or batch, or can be related to the time taken. In the latter case it is sometimes referred to as a *time-saved* system. When this method is used a time is fixed for the job, and the employee is paid for the time saved if he produces it in less then the fixed time. Sometimes he is paid the full amount of time saved, and sometimes a sliding scale is applied giving a varying percentage of the time saved to the employee. Individual incentives are most appropriate where there are lots of people doing roughly the same work, where the operations are individual (e.g. one man, one machine), the output is easy to control and count, where there are mainly short-cycle operations, and where the product is constant in design.

Bonus schemes tend to be used more where the individual's contribution to the total performance cannot be easily separated and measured. Again, various methods are used to decide how much the employee receives, and the main difficulty is in accurately identifying that part of increased production which can be attributed to the employee's efforts and that which is the direct result of managerial action. Schemes which embrace everyone, including top management, tend to avoid this particular difficulty. Supporters of such schemes also argue that as they are linked to the overall success of the organisation, direct and indirect workers can all benefit and it makes them all think more about the factors which make for success. The formula used to measure the total performance enables external factors such as changes in the costs of raw material to be taken into account.

The following are the most commonly used types of individual and group incentives.

Straight piece-work

In straight piece-work a uniform price per piece produced is normally supported with a guaranteed minimum wage. As the price stays constant earnings increase directly with production.

Differential piece-work

The piece-work price is increased when a given output figure is passed. In the United States this is sometimes referred to as the Taylor differential piece rate.

Time-saving schemes

- The 'Gant' method provides for a minimum hourly payment up to 66.6 per cent efficiency, beyond which the rate increases on a graduated scale.
- The 'Rowan' system allots a time for the job and the following formula is used to calculate the 'time-saved' payment:

$$\text{payment} = \text{time taken} + \frac{\text{time taken} \times \text{time saved}}{\text{time allowed}}$$

- The 'Halsey' system gives the employee half the time saved plus the standard time arrived at by work study.

The standard hour scheme

This term is used to describe the system where a job or group of jobs is studied and expressed in standard hours. The employee, or employees, receive the full savings from production above standard.

The Bedaux systems

The job is time-studied, the allowed minutes are converted to points and a specified number of points allocated for the completion of the job. In addition to his basic rate the employee gets a payment equal to 77 per cent of the points 'earned' in excess of sixty per hour multiplied by one sixtieth of his hourly rate.

Group bonus schemes

Group bonus schemes range from the simplest where an amount of money related to output is shared equally among a group to the more complex ones where both the sum to be shared and the proportion going to each employee is the result of complicated calculations which make allowance for all sorts of variable factors.

The Priestman bonus scheme

This is similar to the standard hours scheme referred to above, except that the standard is a pre-determined group, rather than individual, target. A percentage is added to the group's normal day rate according to the percentage above standard achieved. Sometimes output is measured by weight or bulk for this purpose, or it can be converted to points which are then converted to money.

Value added schemes

In value added schemes employees are paid a bonus based on value added. In the engineering industry this was defined by the Engineering Employers' Federation in their 1979 handbook *Business Performance and Industrial Relations* as 'the value added to materials and other purchased items which provides, as a result of productive activities in the firm, the sum out of which wages, salaries and administrative overhead expenses are paid leaving any surplus as profit'.

The Scanlon plan

The Scanlon plan was named after an American lecturer in industrial relations who believed that to be successful a bonus scheme had to cover everyone in a factory from the factory manager to the labourers.

The essential concept is that a bonus over and above normal wages and salaries is paid to everyone in the business, and the bonus is derived from a productivity ratio. This ratio is that of payroll costs to the sales value of production.

The productivity ratio for any given period is set against the ratio as it was in a 'neutral' base or reference period in the past. Once this ratio is determined and expressed then it is applied to the sales value of the production in the current period. The resulting figure is the allowed figure for payroll costs. If present payroll costs are lower than those allowed by the ratio a bonus is payable. If present costs exceed those allowed then no bonus is payable.

If a bonus is payable, one quarter of the amount is set aside as a reserve against periods when payroll costs are more than is allowed.

The remaining three-quarters is split, 25 per cent to the company and 75 per cent distributed to employees *pro rata* according to their wage or salary.

The Rucker plan

This is a variation of the above type of scheme. A more detailed analysis is used to arrive at savings achieved which are then split in different proportions.

Not only can all the above schemes be modified to suit an individual organisation's requirements, but a mix of systems can be used. An example of this mixing used to operate in the aircraft industry. The method adopted provided a time allowance for each job, and this allowance comprised three elements, an estimated standard time, a fatigue allowance and a bonus element. Bonus was paid when the worker saved time out of the total time allowed, at a rate of so much per hour saved in addition to his basic hourly rate. This was, in fact, a generous adaptation of the Halsey system described earlier.

Some companies operate piece-work or production bonus schemes for manual, clerical workers and supervisors, and profit-related bonuses for managers and profit sharing for directors. Some form of performance-related pay for all, even if different systems are applied to different levels in the organisation, is one way of easing the pressures on differentials which inevitably occur if financial incentives are applied to one group only.

4.02 Incentives for indirect employees

Means of improving the performance of indirect employees become more necessary as a way of reducing costs when overmanning and the more obvious direct labour inefficiencies have been overcome. It has been estimated that most indirect workers operate at less than 40 per cent efficiency, so clearly in most organisations there is scope for cost reduction in this area.

Although the first financial incentive schemes were devised for direct manual workers, and in fact piece-work is still largely confined to that group, the need to develop schemes for indirect employees was quickly appreciated. The initial stumbling block was the lack of any credible measuring technique to be used in place of time and motion study, the effectiveness of which had been proved on repetitive operations since the beginning of the century.

While a number of useful approaches had been developed earlier, it was not until the Second World War that analytical estimating of indirect work really developed. There are now a number of well tried methods such as Variable Factor Programming, Group Capacity Assessment, Master Clerical Data, Basic Work Data and Maintenance Data. The various methods are frequently referred to by practitioners and in the literature by their initials VFP, GCA, etc., and most management consultants have their own particular techniques which are usually variations of these. Variable factor programming, which originated in the United States, has been used successfully by English Electric, Phillips, BAC, BOC, and other companies in Britain. The basis of all these techniques is the same as for the techniques used in the study of direct work, namely, observations, timing and recording to arrive at standards. The Clerical Work Improvement Programme (CWIP), a technique designed to control office costs and therefore particularly suitable in organisations concerned about the cost and efficiency of clerical employees, was developed by an Australian firm of management consultants from work done in the United States. Readers need to be aware that some of these methods are covered by copyright, and consultants are often 'licensed' to use them by the originators.

The objection normally raised to using any measurement technique for maintenance work is that the work involves jobs which on the surface appear similar, but which in practice vary considerably in content. One method which aims to overcome this problem uses a time range rather than precise times in setting standards. By using a time range during which it should be possible to complete a job, and using this for all jobs, the differences tend to cancel each other out. The time ranges are arrived at by the time study of benchmark jobs.

Providing the essential ingredients of measurability etc. are present, there are no reasons why one of the well tried incentive systems cannot be linked to an employer's particular target, be he a producer of manufactured articles or a provider of services, or in the private or public sector.

Because incentive plans are associated in most employees' minds with direct workers, and the concept of more pay for more goods produced is easier to understand, indirect employees are usually resistant to incentives which involve measurements of their individual contribution. Convincing them that it is possible, for example, to measure the work of a maintenance electrician or an invoice clerk requires considerable tact and patience, as well as the usual communication skills. Where the plan contemplated is of the group variety, i.e. based on group targets involving direct and indirect workers, the same difficulty does not arise. In these situations problems do sometimes occur, however, due to direct workers resenting the inclusion of those whom they regard as making a lesser contribution. A properly devised and communicated scheme based on total results, such as the Scanlon plan, can overcome such divisions and make all employees understand that everyone has a role to play in achieving the organisation's objectives.

4.03 Using incentives to deal with absence

Although employers normally use incentives as a means of increasing employee effort, they can, of course, be applied to a whole range of problems. Incentives to reduce absenteeism in the form of attendance bonuses are but one example.

The costs of absenteeism are difficult to assess, and clearly vary considerably depending on the nature of the employee's work. In some circumstances absence can result in lost output, poor quality and damaged customer relations, as well as the extra cost of labour used to fill in for the absent employees.

Action taken by employers normally consists of methods to reduce the level of absence which were dealt with in the last chapter, and methods of coping with it when it occurs. These latter may range from simply ringing up an agency to get a replacement typist, to the more elaborate such as creating tasks which can be 'stockpiled' for a pool of trained employees who can then be quickly transferred to fill gaps in moving production lines as they occur.

An employer should only consider using incentives to deal with absenteeism if he has estimated that the costs of absence are significant even after he has pursued a consistent policy of education and discipline.

Absenteeism in most organisations – that is, absence for all causes excluding vacations – normally ranges between 3 and 6 per cent. Most will experience higher levels in the winter months, and fluctuations during the work week, Monday and Friday normally being higher than other days. Where the employees are paid weekly in cash it is normal for absence to be lower on pay days.

If the problem is one of certified sickness absence, the level of income during sickness needs careful examination. Some organisations carry on giving normal pay when employees are off. Others 'make-up' the state sickness benefit to normal pay. Employees off work usually save their travelling expenses and other incidental expenses, such as the cost of refreshments and lunches at work, so that even on an income when sick which is less than their income at work they can be better, or as well, off. This balance will be affected when the employee usually receives extra payments for shifts, overtime, piece-work etc. which cease when he is off; assuming that the sick payment scheme, as most do, provides for pay based on basic pay and not average earnings. Before considering additional payments in the form of attendance bonuses, the employer needs to consider whether the existing sickness payment arrangements provide any incentive or disincentive for the employee to return to work. Concern for employees who are genuinely sick must be carefully weighed in this process, and it may be that special provision is needed for the long-term sickness cases.

If the employer, however, is faced with the difficulties caused by casual daily absence which is not paid for, it implies that the absences are either completely unavoidable, in which case they would not have been prevented by a financial incentive, or the employees were prepared to sacrifice a day's pay to have the time off, in which case a financial incentive needs to be of a significant size to influence their behaviour. If absenteeism is running at 10–20 per cent then, where an attendance pay scheme is operating, an incentive payment will automatically be earned by 80–90 per cent of the employees who would not have been absent anyway. This example illustrates why the costs to the employer of absenteeism need to be carefully balanced against any incentive plan which may result in only a marginal reduction in levels of absence.

To be at all effective, the qualifications for earning an attendance bonus have to embrace all forms of absence. Excluding certified sickness from the disqualifications, which unions will press for, will result in otherwise unauthorised absence being 'converted' to certified sickness. Allowing some forms of absence without loss of bonus will give supervisors or managers the invidious task of making judgements in individual cases, especially those involving self-certification, and will gradually lead to erosion of the qualifications and, consequently, of the incentive effect. The qualification has to be as clear and simple as possible such as a rule on the following lines: 'Attendance bonus will only be paid in respect of any week/month in which the employee was present at the normal starting time and remained, available for work, until normal finishing time on every work day'. Where unconstitutional action is a current problem or anticipated problem such wording could be amplified with an additional clause such as 'Employees will be automatically excluded from participating in the attendance payment plan for any week in which they take part in industrial action, i.e. stoppage of work, overtime ban, go-slow or work to rule'.

To have an equal incentive effect, attendance bonuses need to be related to an employee's base pay. A set money amount of, for example, ten pounds will be less attractive to an employee whose normal pay is three hundred pounds a week than it would to one who gets two hundred pounds. Expressing it as a percentage overcomes this problem but creates unnecessary administrative work. One way round this is for the employer to apply a differential cash payment based on a percentage formula which he uses in his own calculations but does not disclose to employees. This will also enable him to 'round-up' the figure both for convenience and to minimise the cost.

If an employer believes there is sufficient evidence to suggest that attendance bonuses would reduce absence, but assesses that the cost benefits are marginal, he can, of course, consider introducing the bonus at the time of pay negotiations, or when salaries are normally adjusted, and offsetting some or all of the bonus against a pay increase. Although unions regard regular pay increases as an earned right, and resist money with strings attached, it is all money to the employees, and if it is presented in the right way some offsetting is normally negotiable.

4.04 Reducing staff turnover

The cost of losing skilled and experienced employees, like the cost of absenteeism, is difficult to measure, but every employer who has suffered knows it to be an expensive business. The costs of recruiting and training replacements can be calculated fairly accurately. What is more difficult to gauge is the additional time taken to handle problems etc., when years of experience are no longer available.

All organisations recognise the inevitability of some losses, and the prudent ones plan ahead for the predictable retirements, and keep historical records to assess the likely extent of losses through, for example, deaths, maternity and emigration. This does not prevent those losses taking place, but it provides a base for management development, apprentice training and so on. Although no management can avoid the occasional sudden death in its ranks, it can avoid the worst consequences by having adequate replacement plans.

The most common method of paying to retain people is by giving regular increases, normally annually, to keep their pay at a competitive level. Because these increases, or at least the size of them, is subject to negotiations or perhaps an annual performance appraisal, or is even dependent on the fortunes of the business, they are not seen as an automatic reward for service. This leads some organisations to introduce payments linked directly to service. If these are to act as incentives to stay with that employer such payments have to be predictable, i.e. automatic and regular, and additional not substitutional for other pay increases. The most common system is that traditionally used for civil servants and other state employees which gives an increase on an employee's birthday or the anniversary of his commencement of service date. Normally such increments apply where posts are graded and each grade is given a salary scale. The increment scheme is then designed so that an employee can progress through the scale, and his salary at the top will equate with or be close to the bottom salary of the grade above. Variations exist in some organisations providing for automatic progress only to a predetermined point of the scale, progress beyond that being linked to performance or the attainment of qualifications.

When considering financial incentives to keep employees, it is important to understand why people are leaving, and there is no better method than the properly structured 'leaving interview', cross-checked periodically with opinion surveys of those who have already left. A properly structured leaving interview is not the manager calling the employee into his office when he gives his notice in, or on his last day, and asking him why he is leaving. Such questions seldom get a truthful answer. Indeed the insensitive employer or one who regards an employee leaving for another job as an affront is unlikely ever to discover the reasons for people leaving. An experienced interviewer will structure the discussion in a way which encourages the employee to talk about his new job, what he expects to get out of it and leading him to make his own comparisons with the old and the new, seldom asking direct questions about his reasons for going, and rarely asking questions which can be dealt with by 'yes' and 'no' answers.

Although employees do leave because they can get better pay or prospects or more interesting work elsewhere, many who believe they would get such advantages need an impetus actually to apply for another job, take time off to attend an interview, etc. It is this impetus, this reason, which the interviewer is seeking out. It might be simple, an addition to the family that requires more money, a change of address which makes travelling to the present job more difficult or more expensive, or, and this is not uncommon with young office staff in cities where job opportunities are plentiful, wanting to go, or work with, a friend. Sometimes, however, the reasons are something the employer needs to address: feelings of one's efforts not being appreciated, coldness or rudeness on the part of a supervisor, or frustration at the lack of opportunity for training, transfer or advancement.

Because people with the skills to carry out productive leaving interviews are rare, and in any case managements are often reluctant to accept their views, organisations seriously worried about personnel turnover should consider surveying employees who have left them. These will not feel so inhibited about talking about the job they left. A carefully worded letter inviting them to complete a questionnaire, with the added offer to discuss it with them, can produce interesting results. As a 30 per cent response would be a reasonable expectation, this method is likely to be more useful where large numbers are involved.

Some years ago a large employer on Merseyside, faced with big losses of trained workers, conducted such a survey and included interviews which were tape recorded and played back to management. As a result recruitment methods and induction training were modified to meet some of the problems identified. Turnover reduced substantially in the following years.

As most surveys show that the bulk of wastage takes place among short service staff (that is, most people leave within the first one or two years of service), any incentive system which rewards people for long service such as five, ten or fifteen years would not be cost-effective. Unfortunately, giving service pay increments designed to combat this short service wastage, e.g. paying increments only after the first, second and third year of service would not be understood, and would indeed be resented by long service employees. This again emphasises the importance of thoroughly understanding the problem before reaching for solutions. Experience also suggests that turnover is likely to be higher among direct workers than indirect. It was once generally believed that absence and turnover among female employees was higher than among males. While this is still true in some situations, it is no longer true as a generalisation. There is no substitute, therefore, for a thorough analysis. Data about terminations, to be a useful basis for action, needs to be broken down by age, sex, department, wage or salary grade, job category, shift and other factors which may be relevant in a given situation, e.g. the area from which staff are recruited, or the method of travel to work. Payments or other benefits linked to service, which may reduce turnover also often result, unfortunately, in the organisation retaining people it would rather lose. For this reason employers believe that the best way to retain the employees they need is to operate wage and salary structures with sufficient flexibility to reward individual skill and application.

Although pension schemes still act as an incentive for employees to stay with an employer, they are not the influence they were now that organisations are amending their schemes to facilitate the transfer of contributions between funds. Having a scheme which provides benefits above the average, however, can, with a well managed fund, be a cost-effective way of using resources to attract and retain staff. In the full employment conditions which followed the Second World War and lasted until the end of the 1970s, it was believed that only older employees took any interest in pension schemes. Since then the different economic circumstances which have led to many organisations using early retirement plans as a way of reducing manpower have caused a greater interest by unions and employees of all ages.

4.05 Incentives and working conditions

Using money to get employees to accept unfavourable working conditions is a well established practice in many industries, and is likely to continue. Although management's prime aim should be to eliminate hazardous or unpleasant conditions, it is not always possible and employees will, in most circumstances, need motivating to accept them, particularly where the condition is not continuous. Coal miners do not get an allowance or other plus payment for working underground, but expect to have financial recognition for the dirt and danger reflected in their basic wages. A worker, on the other hand, who is not normally subject to extremes of dirt or temperature, for example, would look for some compensation if required to work in such conditions. Where the circumstance is highly unusual and unlikely to be repeated it can be dealt with on a one-off basis. Employers often deal with this informally by giving a lump sum payment, or time off, or both. Where, however, it is a regular, even if not frequent, occurrence then most employers feel more comfortable with some guidelines or criteria to ensure consistency in the way cases are treated.

In establishing a payment policy to deal with these situations they will be concerned to ensure that any payment made is reasonable, i.e. related to the degree of hazard of discomfort suffered, and is controllable. To be controllable, the circumstances in which the payment is made – or not made – require definition. For example, if a maintenance man is required to enter an oven or cupola as part of his duties, it is insufficient to say he will be paid whenever he enters one. Maintenance work may be required when the oven or cupola has just been shut down or at any time between normal operation and when it is cold. Unless these matters are defined confusion will arise as to whether the pay is for the heat or working in a confined space, and other examples of employees working in heat or confined spaces will be cited to support claims.

A similar situation applies if employees are paid for wearing protective clothing. If the incentive is aimed at the wearing of pressurised suits or breathing apparatus or other cumbersome wear, for example, this must be defined. It is a quick, slippery slope between payment for such unusual protective gear and for leather aprons and wellingtons or face masks and nylon boiler suits which are normal wear in many manufacturing processes.

Definitions which enable payments to be controlled need to cover not only the qualifications for payment but the payment itself. The hazard or discomfort being paid for does not usually increase if suffered in overtime or on shift, so there is no rationale for increasing it automatically if the employee's rate is increased by overtime or shift premiums which are usually expressed as a fraction of the hourly rate.

The general rule that payment systems should be seen as fair and be easy to understand applies equally to payments designed as incentives in particular circumstances. In the building trade where most jobs carry some element of dirt, pulling down ceilings was easily recognised as an exceptional condition which qualified for dirt money.

Applying incentives to motivate people to do unpopular tasks becomes more difficult in salaried staff occupations. Because of the more general responsibilities in many jobs it is difficult to define where the normal duties end and the exceptional or additional begin. For example, most senior executives accept that a certain amount of travelling, including being away from home overnight, is part of the job. Middle management would probably also accept this as normal. Supervisors or draughtsmen or accounts staff, however, would not usually hold this view. Often the novelty of travel or staying in hotels is seen as sufficient compensation, and if the employer is not careful to spell out the organisation's rules and principles employees may believe that exaggerated expenses are a part of the incentive. Organisations may motivate employees to undertake extra duties involving travelling and overnight stays in a number of ways. The simplest method is to pay an overnight allowance; a set amount which an employee automatically gets irrespective of the cost of food and accommodation. This is a system used by many road haulage companies for their drivers. The disadvantages are obvious. It encourages employees to get the cheapest accommodation possible or, in the case of drivers, sleep in their cabs. Such practices can be bad for the employer's image, as well as possibly affecting performance. Some organisations pay for travelling time, either at basic or premium rates, but require that all expense claims are properly supported by receipts. Others add a standard overnight allowance to *bona fide* expenses, and others give time off in lieu to compensate for hours above the ordinary spent away from home. A prudent employer will think carefully about how employees are motivated to take on such duties. Assuming that no policy is necessary because a loosely administered system of expenses provides sufficient incentive, could, in the long run, prove a costly solution. An employer who appears to condone excessive expenses might find it difficult to maintain credibility in other efforts to control costs, and indeed might well lead employees to question management integrity in totally unrelated policies.

4.06 Incentives and disputes

In areas of British business such as the motor industry, where the stopping of production by labour disputes was once a daily occurrence, most of the major companies explored ways of using financial incentives to overcome the problem. The most persistent efforts were made by Ford, who still have a supplementary payment for which one of the disqualifications is being 'involved in a strike or stoppage of work whether official or unofficial'. The level of dispute activity, however, is affected by so many factors that it has never been possible to prove statistically whether this scheme acts as an incentive or not. There is anecdotal evidence that it deters employees from short duration stoppages, and is maintained mainly for that reason.

As with unauthorised absence, an employee going on strike is voluntarily forfeiting his pay. It must be assumed, therefore, that to have any incentive effect a plus payment must be sufficient when added to normal pay to influence employee behaviour. As most disputes do not involve all employees, again as with absenteeism, the employer must assess the cost-effectiveness of paying everyone to influence a few. As the majority of employers seldom, if ever, experience a dispute which seriously affects their business performance, it is hardly surprising that such incentive schemes are rare.

4.07 Incentives and working practices

For some years now 'buying out' inefficient working practices during pay negotiations has been the approach adopted by most employers faced with the need to raise labour efficiency. Productivity bargaining, as it has come to be called, is described in a subsequent chapter. Its opponents argue that the one-off payment normally made in such bargains is soon forgotten, unions and employees quickly fail to associate what they received with the changes required by management and, therefore, the incentive effect is short-lived.

An alternative to productivity bargaining often advocated, although the two are not mutually exclusive, is a system of on-going incentive payments, the incentive being a regular payment hourly or weekly to adopt and continue with changed work practices. Unlike productivity bargaining, such an approach involves a change to the pay structure which by definition carries with it all the risks of changing differentials, and remains in place until a further change is negotiated.

If an employer decides to buy improved labour utilisation by this method he needs not only to be clear as to what degree of change he needs but the impact of that on the numbers employed, on supervision and organisation, etc. Only if he is able to project and cost all the effects will he be able to assess the potential savings and, therefore, what might be a cost-effective payment. For example, giving direct workers a plus payment to do all their own quality control should lead to headcount savings among inspectors, but retraining, redundancy or other separation costs will need to be set against these savings. Such changes could lead to the virtual elimination of the quality control activity which might in future merely require someone to do sample checks and maintain statistics. This might involve supervisors and managers and the redesignating of authorities and responsibilities.

Similarly, achieving more flexible working among maintenance craftsmen will probably change the skills required, and involve training for existing employees and changes to the training given to apprentices. As in the quality control example, it could impact on the numbers employed, and the organisation and supervision of maintenance work. Just as with the changes created by the incentive schemes described earlier, the benefits of incentives to change working practices can extend beyond those originally envisaged.

Because payments of this type are sometimes categorised as allowances and not incentives, this should not lead employers to ignore the essential ingredients for success described earlier. Taking short-cuts on the problem analysis or any of the other steps could reduce or even eliminate possible gains. One example is sufficient to illustrate this. If management assumes that the elimination of craft demarcations is totally in the control of the employees concerned they are in danger of missing the fact that in most organisations some demarcations are established by the way management organises the allocation of skilled labour. Recognising this at the planning stage will ensure that provision is made to deal with that aspect in the negotiation, communication and implementation of change.

4.08 Shift and overtime working

Increasingly employers are recognising the advantages of a more flexible approach to working hours. Capital intensive businesses, including those employing white-collar workers on information technology systems, have a need to maximise the utilisation of expensive equipment. In some industries such as textiles, mines, vehicles and chemicals, shift-working is a well established practice, and the compensation for working what others would regard as unusual hours is based on well understood principles. The most common shift systems involving day and night shifts, or early and late shifts, or early, late and night shifts, were traditionally paid for by adding a sum expressed as a percentage, or in money terms, to the normal hourly or weekly rate. In recent years industries such as electricity supply and petroleum have, as part of the process of harmonisation, (i.e. giving manual and staff workers similar conditions) adopted a different approach. The whole system of rewards in the widest sense of pay, hours and status, has been revamped with manual workers given basically the same framework of conditions including guaranteed hours that salaried staff enjoy. The requirement to work shifts has been addressed as part of these conditions. Some organisations, principally those employing white-collar workers, have adopted the flexi-time approach to get or maintain a maximum spread of hours without using plus payments.

Employee resistance to shift working often stems from the conditions which create the need. The practice of working overtime each day or weekends to meet output targets or maintain systems, will often lead an employer to consider shifts as an alternative. Employees who have been enjoying the enhanced earnings generated by this overtime paid at the usual premium rates of time and a third, time and a half, or double time will be reluctant to exchange this for any shift system which does not generate the same earnings.

In such circumstances an incentive to change can be used which can be either a lump sum or in the form of a phased payment, bringing the employee's earnings down in stages from the average overtime earnings to the level of the new shift pay. This also illustrates the importance to employers of keeping overtime working properly controlled. This is best achieved by ensuring that all but emergency overtime is budgeted for in advance and authority to work overtime, even when budgeted for, is vested at a senior level of management. If the employer also defines what constitutes an emergency, and examines each one as it happens with the objective of preventing a recurrence, this will act as an added control.

Chapter 5

Profit-sharing And Employee Shareholding

5.01 Are profit sharing and employee shareholding schemes financial incentives?

Although profit-sharing and employee shareholding are often discussed as if they are one and the same thing, they clearly are not. Some companies operate schemes which reward employees with shares or share options (i.e. an option to buy shares) often on advantageous terms. Others give cash payments related to profits, and others give a choice of cash or shares to employees.

Bonus schemes of the type already described can use company profits as the measure of performance for bonus purposes. They seldom do, however, but use value added or sales or production figures because of the factors affecting profit which are outside employees' control. Most employees, and certainly all unions, understand that the annual declared profit can be, and often is, affected by oil prices, exchange rates, deferred taxes, writing up or down of assets, or other factors over which they have little influence. They are naturally reluctant to tie their earnings to schemes which can be at least partly determined by such factors.

In small companies where the nature of the process and products, the costs of raw materials, customers and prices are well understood, a direct and, therefore, easily recognisable link between employee performance and profits may exist which enables profit to be used as a viable base for an incentive scheme. Such a combination of circumstances rarely exists in the larger business.

Because the employee seldom has direct control over the determination of profits and never over share prices, it can be argued that profit-sharing and employee share schemes are out of place in a book on incentives. Certainly little, if any, evidence exists to prove such schemes on their own improve employee performance. As the Institute of Personnel Management said in its response to a government consultative document on profit-related pay in 1986: 'The pay policy is only part of the culture of an organisation which affects employee attitudes ... ... Profit-based schemes are not intended to provide incentives, their primary aim is to reinforce the culture in which they exist ... Those organisations that have profit sharing schemes can often point to the benefits that accrue from a closer involvement of employees in the success of the enterprise. The organisations that appear in the appendix to the consultative paper undoubtedly are successful and enjoy good relations with their employees. It is noticeable, however, that, in most cases, their profit sharing schemes (and these should be clearly differentiated from profit-related pay schemes) are part of a culture that has been built up over many years and which is based on achieving good industrial relations.' The companies listed in the appendix referred to include Sainsbury, John Lewis, Hotpoint and English China Clay: companies known for their total management approach to employee relations more than just their compensation policies.

Although their value as incentives for improving performance, if they are divorced from other measures to secure employee involvement, is questionable, most employers would recognise the value of profit sharing and employee share schemes as part of an overall plan to gain employee interest in, and commitment to, corporate objectives. They can, therefore, be considered as indirect incentives by employers contemplating more wide-ranging changes in management style as a way of motivating employees.

A survey of employer views of such schemes showed that some companies had introduced them to attract or retain people because companies competing with them for scarce skills had already done so.

5.02 Profit sharing

Any employer who wants to give employees as well as shareholders a share of profits in cash can do so by any method he likes to devise.

He can set aside a sum and divide it equally among all employees, link it as a percentage to individuals' wages or salaries, or use either of these methods but restrict it to certain categories of employees. He can activate profit sharing only when a certain minimum level of profit is reached. Some organisations which operate profit-linked bonuses set aside a share of the profits then use a formula which includes company service, salary grade, a performance rating and a factor based on the individual's contribution to that year's profitability. A well administered annual performance appraisal system based on clearly defined objectives would be a considerable aid if the latter approach was used. None of these methods attract any tax relief either for the company or the employee.

When such schemes are confined to directors or those who are in a position to affect the company's profitability, then they can be classed as performance-related pay schemes. As such they provide a rationale for increasing top level remuneration when efforts are being made to hold down wage and salary increases in the rest of the organisations. Where these bonuses form a significant part of executive earnings they can, however, lead to dissatisfaction in years when profits are down. 'Everyone likes sharing profits, but no one likes sharing losses', applies at all levels. As the recipients are usually paying tax at the higher rates then even in a good year the sum awarded is considerably reduced by the time it gets into their bank accounts. Where the bonus is linked to a group profit rather than the results of individual companies within the group, executives in a subsidiary company which is highly successful can become disillusioned if bonus is repeatedly lost because the group as a whole is not profitable. Where this is a temporary feature the swings and roundabouts results will be more readily accepted. Despite the draw-backs, experience of such schemes suggests they are generally popular with the participants, who usually find the annual lump sum reward more attractive than the same amount would be if divided into twelve parts and paid as an addition to the monthly salary.

Although some organisations which consistently make a profit and regularly pay a share of the profit in the form of a bonus, take this sum into account when doing their annual salary review, bonuses are usually regarded as a plus to be paid on top of competitive wages or salaries.

5.03 Profit Related Pay (PRP)

The idea of giving tax relief on pay increases which were linked to profit was first raised in the 1986 Budget speech, and included in the following year's Budget proposals. The premature closure of Parliamentary business due to a General Election led to it and other clauses being dropped from the first Finance Act. On re-election the proposal, unchanged, was included in the 'new' Budget, and ratified in The Finance (No. 2) Act 1987. The principles are as follows.

An employer wishing to take advantage of the provisions has to apply to have his scheme registered before the profit year starts. The application has to be supported by an independent accountant's report. The main principles are that there has to be a relationship between the profit related pay of a specified unit, or the whole of the business, and the audited profits generated by it. Although new recruits and part-timers may be excluded, at least 80 per cent of the employees must be covered. Schemes must last for at least one year, and when started there must be potential for the profit related element to become at least 5 per cent of total pay. The PRP can be either a simple proportion of profits or a sum which varies in line with year on year changes in profits. For the purpose of the scheme, profit means the profits on the ordinary activities of the unit after taxation as defined in the Companies Act (1985). Although PRP must be determined once a year, payments may be made at lesser intervals, weekly or monthly for example. Half of the PRP up to 20 per cent of employee's total pay or £3,000, whichever is the lower, is eligible for tax relief, i.e. tax relief to the employee. Public sector employees are not eligible

Other requirements are that the scheme must be in writing, the method of calculation has to be defined and once defined cannot be changed, and an annual profit and loss account for the unit covered must be provided.

A special office of the Department of Inland Revenue has been established at St. Mungo's Road, Cumbernauld, Glasgow, and will provide employers with guide notes and application forms.

5.04 Employee shareholding

The concept of giving people shares in the companies in which they are employed has a long history, but had never been a widespread practice in Britain. Such schemes, however, started to gain in popularity in the 1970s and by 1987 it was estimated that schemes which made shares available to all employees existed in over a thousand British companies. The idea has the support of the Conservative Party who regard it as a politically acceptable way of widening property ownership, and the Liberal Party who see it as part of a policy for devolving power and creating co-operation in the community and in industry. The Labour Party is suspicious of the motives of those who advocate it and express a concern, which is shared by others, that encouraging employees to invest their savings as well as their labour in a company is too high a risk for individuals. Employees could lose both their job and their capital if their employer's business collapses. Trade unions at the national level see it as a means of undermining their influence, but trade union representatives at a local or company level are more likely to assess any scheme pragmatically and accept or reject it on the basis of what it is likely to do to employees' total, present and future compensation. Few union officials, national or local, would accept shares as a substitute for hard cash at the bargaining table.

Employers who support the concept do so in the belief that giving employees a stake in the business helps create a closer identity of interests between them and management. Those employers who do not support it usually argue that it leads to claims for an employee voice in the decision-making process, more information about matters which affect profits and share values, and does nothing to offset labour costs. Concerns are also expressed about the views of non-employee shareholders.

5.05 Types of employee share schemes

Employee share schemes can be divided into two broad categories, those which have met Inland Revenue criteria and attract tax concessions, and those that do not. Prior to 1973, tax concessions were confined to executive share schemes. In that year the concessions were extended to include all employee savings-related share option schemes. All of these were abolished when the Labour Government first came to power, and it was not until the Finance Act of 1978 that the concessions now available were introduced. These were added to in the Finance Acts of 1980 and 1984. The 1987 Finance Act made it possible for employees of a company operating an Inland Revenue approved share option scheme and which is taken over to exchange their share options for options in the company acquiring them. The 1978 Act provided tax concessions for schemes which met Inland Revenue criteria, namely schemes that are administered by trustees, which are open to all employees with a minimum of five years' service, and where all employee members enjoy equal terms. In schemes which are approved, shares are exempt from PAYE if held for five years. Capital gains tax is paid at the normal rate on the proceeds from the sale of the shares.

Schemes operated under the terms of the 1978 Act, and subsequent amendments, are normally referred to as ADST, or Approved Deferred Share Trust schemes or some variation of them. An ADST scheme operates by the company allocating a portion of its profit to a trust fund. The fund then acquires shares on behalf of the company's employees. The employee has to hold the shares for at least two years. When the employee sells the shares he pays tax on the selling price or the original fixed price, whichever is the lower. The shares have to be part of the ordinary share capital of the company, or the controlling company if he is employed by a subsidiary. Although the company has some discretion regarding voting rights, the shares must have the same rights to dividends and bonus issues as other ordinary shares, and employees are taxed on any dividends they receive.

The most common variations of ADST are what might be termed mixed schemes where employees may choose as a bonus cash, shares, or a mixture of cash and shares. Generally speaking, and providing the share part of the scheme meets the above criteria for Inland Revenue approval, that part is subject to the same tax concessions and PAYE is paid on the cash bonus as it would be in a normal cash only bonus scheme.

The tax advantage to a company of an ADST scheme, which has had prior Inland Revenue approval, is that it can set against its profits for tax purposes all the payments it makes to the trust fund. To qualify for this tax relief the money paid over has to be used within a specified period for buying shares for eligible employees, or to meet the trustees' reasonable administration expenses.

Under the 1980 Finance Act the Inland Revenue was enabled also to grant tax concessions to Savings Related Share Option Schemes.

Again, to qualify, these schemes must get prior approval from the Inland Revenue, and the main rules are as follows.

The scheme must be voluntary and open to all full-time employees with at least five years' service, and the terms for all employees must be the same. The employee enters into a Sharesave Contract either with a building society or the Department of National Savings. He undertakes to save a specified amount between £10 and £100 each month for a period of five or seven years. At the same time, the employer grants the employee an option to buy shares at the end of the saving period, but at the market price at the time he grants the option. At the end of the period the employee can either buy the shares or take his cash. Any employee wishing to terminate the Sharesave Contract may do so, and the terms depend on how long the contract has run. If less than a year he just gets his payments refunded. If it is between one and five years he gets interest of eight per cent per annum. Between five and seven years he gets a bonus equal to fourteen monthly payments plus 8 per cent for the period over five years. To exercise his option the employee must use the money saved at the appropriate time, i.e., after five or seven years, and then within six months buy the shares.

As in the ADST scheme the shares must be part of the company's, or parent company's, ordinary share capital, they must carry the same rights to dividends and bonus issues as ordinary shares, but the employees do not receive dividends or have voting rights until they have actually exercised their option and purchased the shares. The employees do not pay income tax or capital gains tax on any interest or bonus received from the contract, or on any increase in the share price which might occur between the time of entering the contract and exercising the option. Depending on his individual tax situation, the employee may have to pay capital gains tax if he sells the shares at a profit.

It is possible to design schemes which are even more advantageous to employees by, for example, what is sometimes called *matching*. The principle in such schemes is simply that the employer matches the employee's contributions. If, for example, the employee invests in five hundred pounds' worth of shares, the employer gives him another five hundred pounds' worth. The matching does not have to be one for one, but could be two or more for one. Clearly this is far more attractive from the employee's point of view and, if the prime objective is to encourage employees to buy company shares, has distinct advantages.

In addition to the standards set by the Inland Revenue, the London Stock Exchange has established regulations on employee share schemes which listed companies must observe. The Investment Protection Committee of the British Insurers Association has also published guidelines.

Although schemes approved by the Inland Revenue carry tax advantages, there are a number of non-approved schemes operating in British companies. Most of these were started before the 1978 legislation. Perhaps the best known, the John Lewis Partnership, originated in 1929 when the majority share owner, Spedan Lewis, sold his interests to a trust representing the then existing and future employees. He financed the purchase by a long-term interest-free loan to the trust which administers the scheme to this day. ICI introduced their scheme in 1954, and amended it to take advantage of the 1978 legislation.

Some employee share ownership schemes started with employees buying out an ailing company. In Britain, where the most publicised examples were Meriden Triumph, the motor-cycle company, and the Scottish Daily News, these ventures have not been particularly successful. In the United States, however, where there have been more instances, sometimes with the local community also involved because of the need to save jobs, their record is better. The most noteworthy success in Britain is probably the National Freight Consortium. Previously government-owned, it became a limited company in 1980. In 1982 a consortium of managers and employees bought the company and now over half the workforce own shares.

5.06 Executive share schemes

Share and share option schemes designed to attract, retain and motivate executives are more widespread and have a longer history than schemes open to all employees. The 1984 Finance Act (Amended 1986) introduced tax concessions for executive share option schemes and this led to an increase in the number of such schemes, as well as the amendment of many previously existing ones. One survey estimated that the number of executive share option schemes doubled in the year following the Act. Surveys of executive remuneration also suggest that approximately half of Britain's executives are now covered by some form of share ownership arrangement. Once any employee benefit reaches these levels they become significant as incentives to attract and keep people.

The basic provisions of share option schemes which qualify for tax concessions under the 1984 Act are that an executive pays a nominal sum for the option to buy shares at a fixed price in three or more years time. The limit on such options is one hundred thousand pounds, or four times the executive's salary, whichever is the greater. Salary for this purpose is defined as salary liable for PAYE deduction, and the limit applies to the market value of the shares on the day the option is granted.

One Stock Exchange rule for listed companies is that all employee share schemes have to be approved by shareholders in general meeting. This should restrict attempts to use such schemes as a way of giving excessive payments to directors. A company with institutional shareholders might also be expected to observe the guidelines laid down by the Investment Protection Committee of the Association of British Insurers, the National Association of Pension Funds, the Association of Unit Trust Managers, or the Association of Investment Trust Companies. A case occurred at the beginning of 1987 where a major group had to change its executive share scheme when it 'paid out' options worth eight million pounds to the chairman! Institutional shareholders insisted on tougher criteria for triggering options.

5.07 How valuable are they?

In considering whether or not to introduce a profit-sharing or employee share scheme an employer needs to be clear about his objectives. If other organisations with whom he competes for skilled people have adopted or are planning to adopt such policies he may feel he needs to keep up, both to be able to hire the same quality of people and retain those he has. He also needs to remember that employees and potential employees tend to look at a total job package, i.e. everything they get and everything they are expected to do in return. The absence of such schemes might not be significant if other terms and conditions are attractive. The employer may calculate that for tax or other reasons such schemes are more cost-effective than expenditure on pay or alternative fringe benefits as a means of attracting and retaining the right calibre of people.

If the prime objective is to gain employee commitment he should understand that commitment tends to come through involvement. The degree of involvement achieved through such schemes used in isolation may be minimal, and they might be better added after other steps have been taken to involve employees, such as through comprehensive and on-going communication and consultative programmes. As successful employee involvement is a result of a particular management style this needs to be considered carefully as it may not be compatible with the existing corporate philosophy and culture.

In other words, even though it is arguable whether profit sharing and employee shareholding constitute financial incentives, the same steps of problem analysis, defining of objectives and evaluation of alternatives need to be followed. The temptation to grab at popular or fashionable solutions irrespective of the organisation's circumstances must be resisted.

If the aim is to develop an employee share scheme which would attract tax concessions, then willingness to submit all the data needed to get Inland Revenue approval is a pre-condition to be considered. Willingness to conform to the additional guidelines already described, and to have the proposal discussed at a shareholders' meeting may also be relevant considerations.

In a unionised company the employer has to weigh up the extent to which a profit sharing or share option scheme will lead to greater intervention. Such schemes need not be negotiated provided the employer does not introduce it into wage negotiations as a means of offsetting a pay increase or another claim item. He can just inform the unions and employees of the terms, and make it available on a voluntary basis. Inevitably, however, as time passes the employees and their representatives will take a greater interest in the factors affecting profits and/or the share price. This, in turn, will lead to requests for more information which the employer may not be willing to supply. If he is willing to supply it and wants to make sure it does not get distorted and is properly understood, he might well find himself embarking on a major educational exercise. That might not strike most readers as a problem but in fact, while it is true as a general rule that communications improve relationships, it can also in some instances highlight the different priorities of employees and employers. If the employer is unwilling to concede the claims for more information because of real or imagined fears, the scheme may become discredited and suspicion about the employer's motives will be created.

A thorough evaluation of the cost of introducing and administrating such schemes is essential. Meeting the Inland Revenue rules for approval and the requirements of the other bodies referred to, oblige the employer to have well communicated and documented policy and procedures. Some organisations have rejected proposals for share option schemes because of the administrative effort and costs involved.

5.08 Summary

In summary, if an employer is seeking ways to improve performance by using financial incentives, he is more likely to get results by adopting one of the methods referred to earlier. If, however, the objective is to create a new climate of co-operation, profit sharing and employee share schemes can play an important role if combined with other steps to improve employee involvement. Without such additional steps, and in the wrong corporate culture, or with a style of management incompatible with real employee involvement, they will have no more effect than any other fringe benefit.

There are tax advantages, but these have to be balanced against the employee relations factors, the actions needed to get Inland Revenue approval (and in some circumstances to meet the guidelines of other bodies), and the administrative costs involved.

Chapter 6

Communicating, Negotiating And Introducing Financial Incentives

6.01 The importance of a planned approach

Assuming that the essential requirements described earlier exist, the success of any financial incentive scheme will then rest almost entirely on the extent to which it is understood, the degree to which all employees, including managers and supervisors, are committed to its objectives, and the efficiency with which it is implemented. Research in the 1970s in over sixty companies using incentives also established a clear relationship between the success of individual schemes and the level of consultation which had taken place before and during the introduction.

Because communication, consultation, negotiation and commitment are all interrelated, and some communication must take place almost as soon as the decision to use incentives has been made, the need for an early plan embracing all these aspects is almost self-evident.

Experienced managers will know that communication, whilst it has a part to play, will not by itself change attitudes or create commitment. People may, however, become committed through involvement. The essential difference is that receiving communication is passive, whereas involvement requires a contribution by both parties. It is this giving of ideas and effort–active participation–which helps commit the givers. Unfortunately, too often ideas about management's rights and authority get in the way of real employee involvement.

When beginning to develop a plan, therefore, the first judgement to be made by the employer, or whoever has the responsibility to translate the decision to use incentives into a successful scheme, is about the degree of involvement before, during, and after negotiations or, where negotiations are unnecessary, implementation. His desire to have the benefit of people feeling they own the scheme and avoid the suspicion and even hostility which can result when people feel something is being imposed on them will be carefully weighed against other considerations. Despite the advantages, most executives in a unionised organisation would be reluctant to involve employee representatives in the design of an incentive scheme unless there was a history of successful joint initiatives. Even then it would require careful thought because 'sharing the cake' is the fundamental area of difference between unions and management. Unions' *raison d'être* is getting more for their members, whereas cost reduction is one of management's prime responsibilities.

Most trade union representatives would also feel uncomfortable in such a role, as it could compromise their freedom to criticise the scheme if it did not produce advantages for their members. Employers often forget that unions are by their very nature reactive and not proactive bodies. As a result, union officers and shop stewards prefer to have management make proposals which they can then reject or influence in negotiation. Notwithstanding this fact they will often be highly critical of management proposals, even if only tentative, and protest that they should have been consulted earlier. The union's involvement can start at the negotiating stage, and often it has a very positive contribution to make.

Involving managers, supervisors and other staff who will have a part to play in communicating and implementing the scheme should take place as soon as possible. There are benefits in using at least some of these people in developing the formula which will determine the payment of an incentive, as they would bring to the discussion practical problems not always apparent to the more senior managers.

Changing the way in which employees are compensated, even when the intention is to supplement existing pay levels, probably arouses more interest in an organisation than anything except matters which create fears about job security. For this reason, unless the employer takes and maintains the communication initiative morale could be damaged by rumours and half-truths. Distortions of management's intentions which create unrealistic expectations can be as damaging as fears that management is going to insist on some new and unachievable level of performance. A common management mistake is believing that they have to wait until they have a precise detailed proposal and can answer all the questions before they can start communicating. This is not necessary, and a well thought out plan will recognise this. Using as an example a unionised company introducing a bonus scheme, a simple sequential plan embracing all the features referred to could be as follows:

Day One:
Board approves Working Party proposal that as all essential requirements exist for a successful financial incentive scheme one should be developed and introduced. Letters are sent to shareholders telling them of the decision.
Day Two (a.m):
All management down to and including supervisors are informed of the decision and advised that meetings will be convened to enable them to discuss how the scheme should be constructed and implemented. Supervisors are issued with guide notes for handling subordinates' queries.
Day Two (p.m.):
Employees are told by a newsletter distributed by supervisors that the company has decided to introduce a financial incentive scheme based on sales or value-added or production targets etc., and employees and/or their representatives will be given further information when the detailed arrangements have been worked out/negotiated.

Inform union representatives separately and just prior to the general employee communication, and advise full-time officials by letter.
Day Three:
Convene meeting of departmental heads to discuss how further communication meetings, to include their own staff, should be arranged. Members of Working Party in attendance.
Days Four to Ten:
Meetings involving finance, production, sales, and personnel staff to discuss and develop proposal. Working Party in attendance. Additional working parties set up.
Days Eleven to Twenty:
Working Party meet to finalise formula and administrative arrangements, and draft explanatory letters/booklets for employees. Employees told informally through managers and supervisors that working parties have been set up to work out details of the scheme.

Personnel Manager produces a negotiating plan.
Day Twenty-one:
Detailed formula and negotiating plan submitted to Board for approval.
Day Twenty-two:
Convene meeting with trade union(s) to present detailed scheme.
Day Twenty-three:
Inform all management of outcome of meeting with unions.
Day Twenty-four:
Distribute explanatory letters/booklets to all employees.

Two or more heads are better than one when producing such a plan, as people with different responsibilities will recognise different sensitivities in the workforce and are less likely to forget a group that needs to be included in the communications.

6.02 Communications

A great deal has been said and written in recent years about employee communication, and a lot of valuable experience is available in companies that have adopted an open style of management and been prepared to experiment with different methods. A number of lessons have emerged which are applicable in almost all circumstances.

'Actions speak louder than words.' In other words, what people observe and experience makes more impact than written or verbal communication. For example, employees are more likely to believe that it is necessary to reduce costs if they see executive expenditure on entertaining, cars, etc. being cut back. Messages from above about cost cutting will not be believed if employees see the managing director has a new Rolls or the Board has just voted itself a big increase.

'The medium for relaying messages must have credibility.' If the works' newspaper only ever prints company propaganda and not details of strikes or fatal accidents, for example, anything it says will be treated with suspicion if not derision. If the medium is a person, that person must be sufficiently senior and respected, not necessarily the same things, for what he says to be believed. If the notice boards are only normally used for notices of office dances or copies of the firm's rules, people will seldom read them let alone treat anything there very seriously.

'Messages must be in language everyone understands.' All businesses have their jargon, but generally this is more widely used and better understood by management than others in the same organisation. Using short sentences and one-syllable words where possible and dispensing with jargon is important in getting messages across. Pay is clearer to most people than 'compensation'. Why say industrial action if you mean strike, go-slow or overtime ban? Similarly 'tell' is better than 'inform', and 'ask' is better than 'enquire'. These are but a few examples of how to simplify and thereby make clearer what you want to say.

'Communication is always suspect if it is not the normal practice.' Companies that have a consistently applied policy of open communication find it easier to get messages across for three reasons. They have well tried mechanisms for disseminating information, they build up a depth of understanding about the business, its problems and its objectives, and the openness builds trust and credibility in its messages.

'Interaction between the giver and receiver of messages helps understanding.' So face-to-face communication with the facility to question and discuss can be an ideal way of communicating with employees. Because most people will be inhibited from asking questions or discussing in groups of more than about a dozen, the smaller the group the better. The system of cascading information through briefing groups as advocated by the Industrial Society is based on this principle.

'If a communication vacuum exists someone will fill it.' If there is a lack of information about matters of vital interest then either management takes the initiative or the void will be filled by rumour or by employee representatives putting their own interpretation on the situation.

'There is no such thing as a management secret.' Even if secretaries did not talk to their husbands in bed, in these days of computers, copying machines and white collar unions, there is little that can be kept a close secret in most organisations. Wise managers recognise this and make a virtue of it, adopting an open management style encouraging subordinates to contribute to a wider flow of ideas and experience.

'No matter how much you communicate, if you do not tell people what they want to hear they will continue to say you do not communicate.' There is nothing any employer can do in these circumstances but repeat the message that the accusers apparently do not want to understand, perhaps using different packaging.

Research long ago established that the majority of people only absorb about 30–40 per cent of what they are told or what they read. This absorption percentage, however, goes up significantly when the same message is given verbally and in writing. It does not necessarily mean that even this will surmount attitudinal blocks.

All of these lessons can be applied when communicating about financial incentive schemes to ensure a good understanding of management's motives, how the scheme will operate and the benefits to employees. For organisations embarking on a widespread employee communication programme for the first time, there is now a considerable literature on the subject, and bodies such as the Industrial Society and the Institute of Personnel Management have an advisory service and can supply the names of companies who have experience of putting in communication policies. There are also consultants and others specialising in communication who will for a fee produce booklets, videos, films or complete programmes. Although specialist skills are needed to produce a professional-looking book, film or video, most small companies would not want to go this expense. Providing they are realistic in their ambitions and harness all the in-house skills available, they should be able to produce adequate material. A word of caution, however: the agents who handle a company's product advertising or produce their sales brochures are not necessarily skilled in the techniques of employee communication.

For the company whose size makes it a viable proposition, the face-to-face session in the works or office canteen, or in a hired hall or cinema, has a lot to recommend it. Bearing in mind the seeing plus hearing rule, investment in good slides (a projector and operator can be hired) and a well rehearsed script will improve understanding and give it the touch of competence, not slickness, that employees will respect. Follow basic rules such as ten slides with four lines on each are better than four slides with ten lines on each, relate the script carefully to the slides and do not use figures that are not on the slides (or your audience will stop listening while they search the slide for the figure you have just used), use pictures where possible to illustrate points, keep the language simple, invite your secretary or the office cleaner to attend the rehearsal, and check if they understand it and can follow the slides from the back of the hall. Leave plenty of time for questions and involve all the top managers in giving the answers. If you do not know the answer to something say so. It does no harm to management to show occasionally that they are fallible.

If it is decided to use the cascade approach to meetings, i.e. meetings at different levels addressed by the appropriate level manager, the problem may be encountered of managers who are apprehensive about facing an audience of subordinates, some of whom could be critical of what he has to say. It should be possible to build their confidence by a brief training session which takes them through a rehearsal until they are completely familiar with all the subject matter and practised in handling the awkward questions. One useful by-product of face-to-face communications is that it usually reinforces managers' authority, as they are seen by employees to be knowledgeable and supportive of corporate policy. In larger companies it also enables employees to see the top management who they might otherwise only hear about. Some companies combine this type of employee meeting with a buffet lunch or dinner, and executives use the opportunity to meet and talk to employees informally.

To reinforce face-to-face presentations, employee letters or booklets can repeat all the main points and add detail. Although there are some who argue that the professionally produced booklets complete with illustrations or cartoon figures are more effective, the main purpose is to get the facts across. Given proper thought and care in preparation this can be done as well on duplicated quarto sheets. A little imagination in lay-out can make them look different from other company documents, and the rest is in the words.

The format most commonly used is a statement from the chairman or managing director saying why it has been decided to introduce an incentive scheme. (It is important that this stresses the anticipated benefits to both sides as employees will not believe it is being done for altruistic reasons.) A brief description of how the scheme will work perhaps little more than the formula, should be given, then questions and answers in plain language, not avoiding the more difficult ones. These questions should be drawn up after discussions with supervisors so they reflect the real concerns and enquiries that have emerged.

In employee communications of this type used when introducing share option schemes, it is normal to refer to the legislation and

Inland Revenue rules when explaining how the scheme will operate. If participation in the scheme is voluntary, as it might be if share purchase is involved, then this should also be stressed. When this written communication replaces meetings, it should end up by telling employees how and where they can ask questions and get further information.

In some cases the nature of the incentive scheme or the organisation will make union participation at the communication stage possible. There are then considerable advantages in making statements jointly, either by the union sharing the platform with management at meetings or by signing the explanatory literature. In United States companies that have employee involvement programmes, statements and photographs of senior management and union officers often appear side by side in information news-sheets. The use of photographs helps employees to relate messages to people and can humanise otherwise impersonal documents.

6.03 Involving staff

The two main benefits, in addition to reinforcing communication, which flow from involving people are contribution and commitment – contribution because no one knows more about a job than the person who does it every day, and commitment for the reasons already given. Being asked to contribute views and ideas is an acknowledgement that the employee's knowledge and experience is valued. It seldom fails to make people feel better and more interested in their job, and produce something worthwhile for the matter in hand.

Involving people, however, if it is to produce the best results, requires some skill and arranging. If it is a company's first venture, the chances are that the immediate reaction will be one of suspicion. 'What are they up to? I have worked here twenty years and nobody has ever seemed interested in my opinion before', is not an unusual response to the initial approach. Breaking down that understandable attitude can be a slow but rewarding process, part of which involves convincing people that you are genuinely interested in their views, and it is not just a way of manipulating them.

One technique for overcoming resistance and demonstrating a genuine interest in people's ideas is to construct discussions within meetings, so that views can be put with a degree of anonymity. For example a meeting of a hundred employees could be given a presentation of a problem plus a brief description of the factors that could be causing it. The audience could then be split into eight groups and asked to come up with their views on what are the most important factors affecting the problem. If they are then given time and facilities to talk about it and nominate one of their number to report back a number of things will happen. The cynical and suspicious will be able to include their own ' hostile' questions without anyone knowing the individuals who raised them. An open airing of the hostile questions, if dealt with calmly and openly by the chairman, will help to siphon off the hostility and demonstrate that this really is a change in the way management wants to do things. It will also have led to a better understanding of the problem by all those at the meeting. Given the necessary skill and experience in their handling, such meetings can be developed to move from understanding the problem to developing answers, answers to which those taking part will feel more committed than answers produced by a manager sitting in his office.

Other techniques familiar to many managers include brainstorming, where those in a group are asked to raise any ideas, no matter how wild, about a problem and possible solutions. Usually these are aided by a chairman or recorder who keeps the thing under control, lists the points raised, and focuses the group's attention by the use of a blackboard or flip charts. This is a useful way of getting examined what might otherwise be considered unusual proposals. Sometimes the unusual idea which might not see the light of day in a more formal meeting because it could seem too 'way-out', contains the basis of a solution or leads to an examination of facets of the problem previously overlooked. There are also more systematic methods which include problem analysis, decision analysis, analysing potential problems which may arise from alternative decisions and applying weighting factors at some stages. Either of these techniques could be used with any size of meeting by employing the seminar group approach.

When introducing a financial incentive scheme into an organisation with no experience of employee involvement, the involvement is best confined to those employees management feels are already sufficiently committed to make an immediate positive contribution. The first part of the process following the decision to use incentives, where some degree of involvement is valuable, is in writing the definitive formula which will determine the incentive payments. If the scheme decided on is a plant or company-wide bonus plan, then it is reasonable to assume that some broad or tentative formula was drafted, or at least discussed, when the decision was made. This will need converting to a clear and accurate statement of the scheme, i.e. management's objective. A group representing the key functions, but not necessarily confined to the heads of those functions, could be ideal for this purpose. In all but individual or small group bonus schemes this group will need to have sufficient data about previous performance levels to be able to set a valid standard. For an incentive scheme that means a standard which is achievable but does not result in extra pay costs without extra performance – in other words, a formula which ensures that incentive payments are cost-effective.

It is at this stage that the group will set down precisely what will qualify for incentive pay and what will not, determining the extent to which improvements created by investment in new machines, processes or designs result in bonus payments, and introducing the qualifications to protect the quality of product or service. The refined formula could then be debated by a wider group until all of management is satisfied that it represents an economic, workable, understandable and, if necessary, negotiable basis for the scheme.

If the incentives proposed are related to the performance of individuals, as for example are most piece-work systems, or related to the performance of groups within the bigger workforce, then the process of definition will need to be more devolved. Departmental managers, supervisors and work study engineers will need to examine the scheme for its potential effects job by job, or group by group, to set valid standards. Here again the task will be helped by involving all those who can contribute. Time-office staff, for example, who are often recruited from the ranks of manual workers and who process much of the workshop level records, can prove invaluable in pointing out potential administrative problems or loopholes in the control process. Quality control and material handling staff also will often identify flaws in what looks like tightly controlled incentive schemes.

As a general rule, incentives paid to individuals or groups for parts produced off a machine, or assembled in a section, or forms processed in an office, which are just part of a longer process or system, require for more control data than schemes which relate to the performance of a whole organisation. Inadequate control of work in process, for example, can soon lead to counting the same units twice for bonus. Slackness in the handling of scrap or reject pieces can have the same result. The writer was once involved in disciplining a supervisor who had his own set of rubber stamps made to increase the number of O.K. jobs recorded on his shift.

Employers should not be deterred by the need for a comprehensive recording system. As stated earlier, the cost of administration is one of the factors that must be weighed when considering incentives, but indirect benefits often follow from detailed information becoming available for the first time. This flow of data on a regular basis, if used wisely, can provide insights into scrap costs, machine performance, material standards and manning imbalances, enabling cost reductions to be made over and above those generated by improved labour performance.

Having a scheme which relates payments to some simple and easily measurable base, such as number of units delivered to customers, avoids many problems and does not need the same degree of involvement to gain employees' contribution to its design and implementation. Commitment and understanding, however, the other benefits which come from involvement, are important in all incentive schemes.

The need for communication and involvement does not end once the scheme is running. Interest needs to be sustained by regular reports on its progress. This is even more important if falling sales or other economic changes are likely to affect incentive earnings. Employees need to know if factors within or without their control are impacting on the scheme's results.

6.04 Do incentives have to be negotiated?

This question will normally only arise in companies that have an agreement or a moral commitment to negotiate changes to conditions of employment with unions or other bodies, such as a joint representative council. Where it is customary for the management to announce changes to employees, this could apply equally to introducing an incentive scheme. Even where changes are normally negotiated, introducing an incentive scheme which does not reduce existing rates of pay or affect earnings differentials, and which clearly will not substitute for negotiated pay increases, does not necessarily have to be negotiated. Unions will argue that any incentive, even if paid as a plus to negotiated rates just like regular paid overtime, will boost earnings and thereby over a period enable the employer to get employees to accept lower base rates. Although there is obviously some truth in this contention, as far as the employer is concerned it is all pay and if he can increase employees' earnings without putting up his labour costs by making some of that pay performance related, it makes good business sense to do so. Employees are not usually too bothered about how their pay is calculated as long as they believe it is a fair return for their skill and efforts, and it is sufficiently consistent for them to feel they have some security of earnings.

In most circumstances where pay and conditions are negotiated, incentive schemes will also involve some degree of negotiation. How much will depend on the type of scheme, the amount of employee co-operation needed to make it effective, and the influence of the union or unions over the employees concerned. As a general rule the extent of negotiation needed will be related to the criteria for earning incentive pay. Where pay is related closely to the efforts of unionised employees, such as with traditional piece-work or gang bonuses, the unions will want to negotiate that criteria in some detail and probably have an active on-going role. Where incentive pay is linked to overall company performance, their involvement might well be limited to one meeting where the operation of the scheme is explained and with the unions reserving their right to re-open discussions on an as and when needed basis. This would probably be the situation where employee share option schemes are launched.

In organisations where a majority of the employees are members of unions, and those unions have agreements giving them nogotiating and procedural rights, they will invariably insist on negotiating the terms of any incentive scheme where their members' efforts are the main criteria for getting plus payments.

6.05 Planning the negotiations

As with any planning, it is a good discipline to start off by writing down the objective, in this case what result the employer wants from the negotiations. The statement needs to be clear on a number of issues, the most important being the parameters within which a settlement would be acceptable. If the intention is to negotiate and not force the employer's plan unchanged on the workforce, then the negotiable and non-negotiable areas need to be understood by the employer, and whoever represents him at the negotiations. For example, cost calculations may show that the scheme breaks even, i.e. all the costs including extra pay for employees equals the gains to the company of increased income, when employees' 'share' or bonus under the formula reaches 70 per cent. In these circumstances the employer might well decide that the risks associated with putting in the scheme are not worth taking unless he is averaging 10 per cent better than break-even. Therefore, any change to the formula which allows employees to earn more than 60 per cent is non-negotiable.

The employer may also, for example, decide that once it is set he cannot afford a change to the formula within the forseeable future. Any claim from the unions, therefore, that the formula should be re-opened for negotiation, either at predetermined intervals or in certain circumstances would be non-negotiable.

Just as war is the extension of diplomacy, so the strike is the extension of negotiations. Most companies planning to negotiate an incentive plan will feel confident that a strike is only a remote possibility. Despite this they still need to consider their reaction to such an unlikely event. If, because of market conditions or other reasons, they could not take even a short strike, those handling the negotiations need to know that. It is a factor which must be taken into account when planning any negotiation, but obviously never disclosed to the unions. One of the few circumstances where an employer might include a strike as part of his negotiating strategy is where he is convinced he can get a better settlement after a strike than without one, and the objective is important enough to risk the damage to employee, customer and public relations, and other costs which will result. In this case a careful evaluation of the possible strike cost would form part of his total plan.

Because the majority of employers will do everything possible to reach a peaceful and harmonious settlement with the unions representing their employees, their negotiating plan will reflect this. They will deliberately construct their initial proposals to allow the unions to demonstrate some gains. The most successful negotiations are those where both sides leave the table believing they have achieved some change in the other's position. The emotions generated by a strike, and the damage it does to the employer's business and employees' income usually destroy the chances of such a settlement.

It is during this early stage of the planning that management will need to make the best assessment it can of the union's and employees' objectives. For the reason that unions understand that in the last analysis they draw their power from the employees, and whatever is negotiated has to be acceptable to them, the objectives of unions and employees will largely coincide. The main difference wil be that the union will also tend to look at the management's proposals in the broader and longer term context, such as their possible effect on future negotiations, numbers employed, etc.

How management sets about this task of assessing all these ideas, aspirations and objectives will depend a lot on the size of the organisation and sources of information. In large unionised organisations there are normally frequent formal and informal contacts between representatives, full-time officials and different levels of management. Well developed lines of communication will enable the employer to collate views from supervisors, personnel officers and managers who talk to union representatives and employees. Experience will teach the employer to evaluate the reliability of the sources as well as the information, and then apply his own judgements. In smaller organisations where the employer has frequent, perhaps daily, contact with the majority of his employees, the job is much easier, but it is still important to listen to others' views, such as those of the supervisor and any colleagues. Some of the biggest mistakes in negotiations are made by employers who believe that they know all there is to know about their employees' views. They are often shocked and sometimes even hurt by discovering that they do not share the same ideas about the matters being discussed.

In most circumstances employees will welcome the chance to earn the extra money provided by an incentive scheme. The exception will be when employees feel that meeting the scheme's requirements will impact in an unacceptable way on other features of their job. Any scheme which involves men competing against each other where previously friendship and co-operative effort prevailed would fall into this category, as would a scheme which required employees to move within departments where employees also prized the ability to form permanent working relationships. Although money is always high on the list of employees' objectives, it is only one of many things they look for in their working environment. The message here for those evaluating employees' objectives for negotiating planning purposes, is that they should be alert to aspirations and concerns which are not always apparent on the surface. Even measures which the management introduce as part of the scheme for the benefit of employees can cause suspicion and resentment if not properly understood. Asking employees to sign for things is an example of a requirement which can cause such difficulties. An employer may see this as a method of protecting the employee and assuring that his responsibility is defined and limited, but the employee may see it as a device for allocating blame and imposing a quasi-legal responsiblity which goes beyond the terms of the usual job contract.

A union's objectives in any negotiation can be broadly split into the economic and the non-economic. Some would describe the non-economic as power objectives, but they would usually be more accurately described as role objectives which are about maintaining the union's ability to represent and protect its members. Where the union representatives doing the negotiating are also employees, as will often be the case, one cannot ignore the influence of personal interest on their arguments. It would be an unusual shop steward who did not work out what any incentive scheme might do to his own earnings.

The union's economic objective will obviously be to get as much money as it can for its members. Union representations will be concerned that the formula reflects conditions which can be influenced by employees, that it is written in a way which gives employees the lion's share of gains generated by employee efforts, and that it gives a reasonably consistent level of reward. In addition they will have views about differentials and generally want to maintain them. If they are dissatisfied with existing differentials, they may hope the incentives provide a means of achieving the changes they want. This could well be the case with unions representing semi-skilled workers who believe the skilled differential is too large. Where the supervisors are in a white collar union they might fear a narrowing of their differential. The employer will need to evaluate the strength of these sectional interests within the broader union objective, and how they are likely to impact on the negotiations.

Union representatives experienced in the working of incentive schemes will be concerned about their divisive nature, particularly when the formula allows wide disparities of earnings between different groups. Aware that as far as their members are concerned their main job is to protect and increase earnings, they will be suspicious of any scheme which removes a significant part of earnings from the bargaining table. Conversely they will also recognise their limited power to resist anything which promises attractive rewards for their members.

Two of the union's major objectives will be to have a hand in determining the standard in the formula, and an on-going right to question its interpretation. Both of these will result in demands for all the information necessary to understand how the standard is established and subsequently measured. To be effective as an incentive, everyone needs to understand the formula and trust the way it will be implemented. The employer should have no objection to supplying this information

Once those responsible for planning the negotiations have done the basic ground work and made a reasonable assessment of the aims of their workforce and their representatives, they will need to commit a plan to paper. Not only will this provide the material for a definitive proposal to be put to the board for approval, but will also prove a useful discipline and guide for those doing the negotiating. Perhaps the best way to do this is to write down how the proposed incentive scheme will look in agreement form, setting out the formula, employer's, employees', and union's role and responsibilities, administrative principles, rights to information, procedure for querying interpretation, etc.

If all these areas are listed in paragraphs which capture the employer's objectives, then the union's objectives can be put alongside in a separate column. A column can then be added showing the employer's 'permissible' area of negotiation. (In wage and salary negotiations a final column would also be included showing the cost of conceding each particular part of the claim.) The following is an example of how an extract from such a planning paper might read.

Draft plan to negotiate a financial incentive scheme at the XYZ Manufacturing Company's Leicester factory

Introduction
At the board meeting on 20.8.87 it was decided to introduce an incentive plan based on production targets at the Leicester works. It was agreed that this would be confined to manual workers. Incentive schemes for clerical, administrative and supervisory grades are being considered separately. Our agreements with the three unions representing manual workers require us to negotiate. It states 'changes to basic rates, shift and overtime premiums and any change to the method of calculating the remuneration of employees represented by the signatory unions will be the subject of negotiation at the Joint Works Council'.

Objective
To negotiate a bonus scheme which will give manual workers a bonus related to output which results in higher output and savings in unit labour costs.

'Agreement' language	*Union/employee objective*	*Negotiability*	*Notes*
Eligibility			
'All full-time adult direct and indirect male and female employees on the weekly payroll of the Leicester works'.	Part-time employes on a *pro-rata* basis and employees assigned week by week from Coventry.	Concede part-timers if necessary for a settlement. Including Coventry-loaned labour could lead to claims for a similar scheme there, where studies have shown it would not be viable, so must be resisted to point of strike if necessary.	Accounts would be unhappy if part-timers are included, believing administrative costs of inclusion, because of labour turnover, are not worthwhile.
	Craft unions may press for apprentices over 18 to be included.	Reject – our apprentice rates are over-competitive.	
Calculation of bonus			
The bonus payable will be 50 pence for each 100 units cleared by Inspection Dept. over	'More for less'. The unions will aim for a penny per unit. The right to challenge	The best assessment from Cost Accounting is that 65–70 pence is the break-even point. The	To give more negotiating flexibility we could open at 45 pence. Anything below this

'Agreement' language	*Union/employee objective*	*Negotiability*	*Notes*
the weekly average of units delivered in the standard period.	Inspection Dept's decisions to reject batches.	board believe we should drop the scheme if we cannot hold the payment at 60. Reject – if it looks like becoming a breakdown issue agree to *notify* TU side of Works Council of reasons when rejection rate exceds 15% per cent.	lacks credibility at the table. Production management would not be averse to union involvement on quality problems in some departments.
The standard period for this purpose will be the last full working week in June 1984.	They will probably argue for another period knowing this 26-week period was our best production run for four years.	Every month the period is moved back costs the same as a penny per hundred on the bonus.	Putting money on the bonus will give more 'negotiating mileage' than altering the period.
Payment of bonus			
'Bonus where earned will be paid monthly in arrears and will not be included in the calculation of shift or overtime premiums, sick pay or vacation pay.'	Include an average bonus in holiday pay.	No bonus except as a result of extra output is a principle we must hold for as long as possible. We should drop our proposal before conceding in these negotiations.	They can probably be bought off of this with other concessions.

	Have a percentage of bonus payable in every period put aside in a pool to distribute in periods when no bonus is generated.	Delaying a part of the bonus will detract from the incentive effect. No negotiating flexibility on this point except as shown in note.	If this becomes the only point stopping a deal we could agree to review it at the end of the first year's operation of the scheme.
'Employee representatives on the Works Council will be provided with monthly output figures and quarterly figures showing bonus paid in the previous three months.'	Weekly figures of output and bonus.	This can be conceded but only if it is useful to do so during negotiations.	The amount of extra administration is negligible but convener is collecting earnings data on a weekly basis in preparation for next wage claim.
'There shall be no attempts to influence the level or distribution of bonus by strike, overtime ban or work-to-rule and in the event of such action being taken all employees covered by this agreement shall be disqualified for bonus for any week in which such action occurs.'	The unions will want to abolish this clause and replace it with some toothless words of assurance.	This or a very similar clause is a management must because of past experience at the Leicester works. Only one of two areas of negotiability – limit the penalty to the department involved or to a *pro rata* of the week's bonus – not both.	

Although success in negotiations is related to the amount of thought that is put into the planning of the negotiators' objectives and manoeuvrability, the negotiations can still be lost if the case is not presented in the best way and in the right atmosphere. Planning, therefore, should also embrace the selection of the team and time and place of negotiations.

The composition of the negotiating team may be predetermined by the size of the organisation, the balance of power within management, the areas of interest of different managers, or simply just custom and practice. Where these limitations do not exist selection should be based primarily on two factors, the knowledge and skill individuals bring to the table, and here skill means skill in relationships, and their importance in 'owning' the results of the negotiation. In the negotiation of a clerical workers' incentive scheme, for example, it would be essential that the executive responsible for the efficiency of clerical effort (e.g. the man in charge of administration) was part of the negotiating team. If the negotiation is about a production-based bonus for process workers, then the production director or production manager should be involved.

These individuals need not take the lead part in the dialogue with the unions, but must be present to make their contribution either as advisers during the meeting or as participants during adjournments. The number of people only matters as far as the other side will feel obliged to match it. What is important is that there is a clear understanding of people's respective roles. The best method is where each side nominates one spokesman and others only join in if invited to do so by him. Differences of opinion, compromises on points and disputes about facts should be dealt with by each side in separate adjournment discussions so as not to expose areas of weakness to one's negotiating opponents. A mistake made sometimes by both unions and employers is to field a side which has status but lacks the detailed practical knowledge of the matters under discussion. A competent junior manager can often be of more use in a team of negotiators than a board director, and a shop steward more valuable than a national official. The successful lead negotiator is one who commands the respect of his own and the other side by virtue of his grasp of the theory and practice of the policies involved, an understanding of his own mandate and the extent to which this can be stretched to achieve a settlement, a sympathetic understanding of his opponent's points and an ability to listen as well as instinctively counter points of arguments which must be countered, and ignore those which do not. Contrary to popular belief the good negotiator does as much listening as he does speaking, and needs to employ his skills as adroitly with his own side as with his opponents.

Thought also needs to be given to the timing of negotiations. If participants have long journeys to make to the venue then both starting and finishing times must accommodate this, or the dialogue could be interrupted at delicate points by late arrivals or early leavers. If it is clear that the amount of material to be presented and discussed will need some hours, then it is better to schedule a number of meetings rather than attempt to cram everything into one day. Getting an agreement on something which may last for years is worth an investment of time, even by the busiest manager. If they cannot afford the time the negotiations may be more successful without them. In planning meetings even the timing of an interruption for serving tea or coffee should be considered. Presenting a complex paper which has been drafted to enable a logical sequence of argument to be followed can be ruined by the distraction of teacups being passed around the table. Equally, trying to force a conclusion to difficult arguments when key participants are beginning to look at their watches and calculate the time it will take to catch the next train can be disastrous.

If it makes sense to have more than one meeting, the planner should think through the objectives of each meeting separately, recognising among other points that the parties will be open to outside influences in the intervening period. Where it can be done without damaging the outcome of the negotiations, this period can be used for communicating progress to employees and judging their reaction to the company's proposals. The experienced negotiator will use these breaks between meetings as productively as he uses the adjournments within meetings. Sometimes the stance taken by the other side will cause him to reappraise his total strategy and require a new negotiating plan. If the initial analysis was correct, however, his position on fundamental points will not alter.

Choosing the venue for meetings is normally a choice of using the organisation's own premises or hiring other accommodation. The basic requirements are quiet and privacy, separate adjourning rooms for each side, an office with telephones where back-up staff can prepare new arguments or check statistics, and telephones for both sides to use to take messages, etc. Where premises are being used for the first time other facilities, like car parking, toilets, catering etc., should be checked out beforehand, as well as the acoustics in the meeting room. Common hazards when using hotels are the clatter of cups or cutlery, or the hum of vacuum cleaners interrupting speech and deliberations, or the bustle of staff or guests interrupting critical telephone calls. The writer recalls one occasion when during a meeting arranged at short notice to prevent a strike which could have cost millions of pounds, managers dashed around looking for coins so they could use a conference centre's pay phones which did not take incoming calls. Clearly there are considerable advantages to holding negotiations on your own premises if the necessary accommodation and facilities can be made available.

6.06 Handling the negotiations

When the management has refined the statement of objectives and considered its negotiability it is customary to have this agreed by the board. It is important that the board also understands and accepts the limits of negotiability and the point at which the choice may have to be made between abandoning all or part of the objective or taking a strike in a further attempt to secure it.

A well thought out negotiating plan will largely determine how the negotiations themselves should be handled. In discussions about financial incentives there are often advantages in starting off by explaining the process of thought that led to it being proposed – perhaps a brief presentation on the company's trading position and prospects, followed by an explanation of why and how it is believed an incentive plan would help. The employer would be well advised to adopt a joint problem-solving approach in negotiations of this type, emphasising the common interest in what is proposed. Using people not normally associated with negotiations at this preliminary stage has some advantages. The person who chaired the Working Party might be a suitable choice if he meets this criteria. It will help to create a different and hopefully less adversarial, climate for the discussions which follow, and is often very useful to the individual concerned who perhaps will be facing hostile questions on the scheme for the first time.

The next logical step would be to explain the scheme but without putting any figures to the money proposed, and inviting questions on the mechanics of how it might work in practice. The aim would be to get a good understanding of the formula and how it would operate, and seek agreement in principle to its introduction. The most likely union reaction would be a statement that they would agree the priniciples but acceptance depends on the money being right. They might, in fact, even suggest a figure at this point, but probably one intended to start the bidding rather than a proposal they expect to have agreed. It is more likely that they will press the company to 'spell out' the figures.

If the employer has done his planning, including the best costing he can, then it is just a question of how quickly he arrives at his final 'offer'. Depending on all the circumstances, the usual negotiating rules regarding offers should apply. The first offer needs to be low enough to leave maximum scope for negotiation, but not so low that it is obviously not meant to be regarded as serious. Too many steps between first and final offer can irritate and even be dangerous, making the other side believe they only have to sit there saying no long enough for it to be gradually inched up to an acceptable figure.

In most negotiating situations there are other variables in addition to money, and these should have been identified in the plan. If the scope for moving on money is limited, then the employer should move the dialogue to these other areas, but in a way which leads the unions to press for concessions and not in a way which makes it appear he is anxious to offer them. An experienced negotiator can trail a coat without the other side knowing he has taken it off.

During negotiations, listening to and observing the other party are important aids to understanding their strengths, weaknesses and aspirations. It is a mistake to believe that everyone who is part of a negotiating team, be it the employers or the union's group, have identical objectives. Facial expressions and other signs of irritation can indicate when the spokesman is not voicing the views of others. Again, an experienced team with proper disciplines will conceal any differences until they are in adjournment. Using the negotiation of an incentive scheme based on the performance of small working groups as an example, the representatives of skilled men may have very different ideas from the representatives of direct workers. It is important to the employer to agree a scheme which all the unions will support, and the areas of sensitivity may only emerge at the negotiating table when the representatives begin to understand for the first time how the scheme will operate. If their differences do come out into the open, or are just indicated by people's demeanour, the employer needs to feel out the ground very carefully, perhaps taking an adjournment to consider what may to him be new factors. It is much better to have a number of meetings to enable proper consideration to be given to the situation as it develops than hurry through to complete a deal at one sitting. This is particularly true where new concepts, such as introducing new ways of rewarding people, are involved.

If the negotiations are spread over a period then some thought needs to be given to employee communications. Unless it is customary to communicate while negotiations are in progress it would be best to agree with the unions how it should be done. In most cases a brief notice or a message passed down by the supervisors to the effect that 'discussions have been adjourned', 'will be resumed next day or week' etc., will be sufficient.

At the conclusion of the negotiations it is vital to make sure that everyone taking part has a common understanding of what has been agreed. If the discussions have been prolonged and have perhaps reached a late hour, people will be relieved that they are over and anxious to get away. Despite this the employer should prepare a statement which captures all the main points and read it out. The main points will include who is covered by the agreement, how it will work (i.e. the formula), when it will take effect (and terminate if appropriate) and what the process is for raising questions and problems about it in the future. He should then get the union's agreement as to how this will be set out and formally agreed. Although a few small companies still operate quite satisfactorily with only verbal agreements, the normal practice is either an agreement written in formal language and signed by both parties, or an exchange of correspondence proposing, describing and accepting the terms.

Chapter 7

Implementation And Monitoring The Results

7.01 Getting ready for day one

Before the negotiations, or announcement date when no negotiations are involved, it is important that someone has responsibility for ensuring that the scheme can be implemented. This can be a simple matter of just ensuring that when a sales figure has been reached or value added hits a target point a payment is calculated for each employee and added to his wage or salary. In most cases, however, more than that is required. Calculation of the formula or measuring individual or group performance will require new information or information produced in a different form.

Simple or complicated, someone needs to sit down and think through just what will be required to translate a proposed or negotiated scheme into action. If the scheme will run on computerised data a programme has to be written, and methods of transferring raw data on to the computer devised. Whether computerised or not, someone has to examine existing data recording methods to ensure they are adequate, or design changes to forms etc., to accommodate whatever is needed for the scheme. A simple example of the type of modification that may be required is that to accommodate absence. Where full pay for sickness is the policy, salaried staff payment systems often operate on an exclusion basis, i.e. salary is paid automatically each month into employees' bank accounts as long as the employee is on the payroll. A bonus scheme which paid out monthly but did not include payment for periods of absence might require a change to the normal salary payment system.

Not only is time required for writing a computer programme or printing new forms for recording output etc., but everyone involved in the scheme needs to understand how it will operate in practice. Accounting managers, wage and salary clerks, ratefixers, supervisors, quality control staff and many others may have to be trained in the new system. Planning ahead will pay dividends.

7.02 The role of the unions

In an organisation where a majority of employees are union members, the union is likely to take an on-going interest in the scheme.

Although the unions' prime objective will be to maximise incentive earnings, clearly this can also be in the employer's interest if the scheme has a sound base. It would not, on the other hand, be in his interest where the unions are able to challenge the formula, claiming it or its interpretation is the reason for 'low' earnings. In these circumstances the scheme is more likely to be the cause of conflict than of higher productivity.

It is because of such risks that some employers insist on the unions' rights in an incentive scheme being spelt out in the agreement. A clause which prohibits attempts to challenge or renegotiate any terms of the scheme during its life are a useful safeguard. Apart from protecting himself in this way the employer could also define in a restrictive way when and in what circumstances problems could be raised by employees or their representatives, and the procedure to be used for this. This latter clause could, for example, restrict the raising of problems to the period when economic matters were normally negotiated and/or confine the right to deal with such problems to a joint works council, or full-time union officials to reduce the risks of sectional interests being pursued.

In organisations with a history of poor industrial relations, a clause suspending the scheme during periods of strikes or other action might also be appropriate. The majority of employers, however, would find such agreement clauses unnecessary and unhelpful.

Where a scheme has been negotiated, union representatives will normally become so knowledgeable about its workings that they will be seen by employees as authorities and expected to handle questions and disputes about interpretations. In schemes related to individual or 'gang' performance which is variable in nature, their role will often extend beyond this and they will negotiate piece-work rates or bonuses with a ratefixer, supervisor or manager. In organisations where there are strong representative structures, almost any variable element of pay, including merit, will become the subject of negotiation unless the criteria for payment are generally understood and accepted and are tightly controlled.

In most circumstances the unions' role will be supportive, supplementing other ways of explaining the scheme and its workings to employees. In many organisations with a stable, well established system of consultation and representation, union representatives act almost as an extension of the personnel or welfare department on fringe benefit matters such as sick pay and pensions, and can fulfill a similar role in advising on and interpreting the incentive scheme to employees. In others the unions' role is strictly confined to handling employee grievances and in some they have no role at all. Where circumstances create only an adversarial role the unions will probably treat the incentive scheme as another management policy to be attacked and eroded. Only the reader will be able to judge the unions' likely role in his own situation.

If the employer wants to confine the role of the union, in addition to making sure this is covered in the agreement he should look at employees' needs for advice and information and provide for it through management channels. In some organisations employees go to their union representatives because experience teaches them that they are more likely to get the help or advice they need from them than from their supervisor. Employers can, therefore, unwittingly build up support for unions by ignoring employees' needs and not providing supervisors with the information and resources to handle their subordinates' problems. This is another argument for communications and training as part of any pre-launch programme on incentives.

7.03 The advantages of a trial period

If the incentive scheme represents the organisation's first venture into performance-related pay, then there has to be an element of the unknown even in the most carefully thought out plan. There is some value, therefore, in having a trial period during which all aspects of the scheme can be monitored and mistakes in administration etc. rectified. If the employer wants to have the facility to abort the plan on a specified date at the end of the trial period this possibility will need to be made known to employees from the beginning, as well as the basis on which the decision will be made. Because schemes can lead to escalating costs, where they are negotiated the agreement should always have a termination or review date so the employer is not committed to the scheme *ad infinitum*.

Even where the scheme has not been the subject of negotiation and no trial period is specified, common sense dictates that, unless there are compelling reasons for doing otherwise, incentives should be introduced into normal or average operating conditions. Periods of high demand for the organisation's products or services, or of significant changes in process or products, may lead to inflated or deflated levels of incentive earnings, making it difficult for both the employer and the employees to judge the scheme's effect. Such a start could dampen the incentive value and demoralise employees or, conversely, lead to exaggerated expectations.

7.04 Audits

For an objective review of the scheme the employer will need sufficient information to measure its cost-effectiveness. This will ideally include not only data to relate performance and earnings at appropriate intervals, but also information about other factors which could have influenced them, such as extreme weather conditions, strikes, breakdowns, or currency fluctuations. Only by separating out other influences will he be able to make valid judgements about the incentive. Here again there is value in a working party approach to the evaluation to ensure greater objectivity. Managers responsible for suggesting incentives, and one assumes enthusiastic supporters of that method of improving performance, may be less than impartial in weighing up the results. Again, facts – not assumptions – are the raw material of effective analysis.

Where the scheme in operation depends on measurement of performance at individual employee, section, or departmental level, it is worth considering building in checks as a regular part of any internal audit system. Frequent and regular examination of performance and earnings figures is more likely to identify anomalies and irregularities than infrequent one-off type checks. It also enables those doing the audit to become more familiar with the system and recognise when it is going wrong. Needless to say, those doing the checks should be knowledgeable about the organisation's policies, practices and procedures, and should not be beneficiaries of the scheme.

The Post Office's Improved Working Methods scheme, which pays a bonus based on savings achieved in overtime or manning, is monitored regularly. Each Head Post Office monitors the scheme's operation in its own area and reports the results to its Regional Office. The Regions carry out regular checks in addition to the checks carried out as part of the internal audit department's programme.

An audit team will, in particular, be looking for any indications that the standard has been set too high or too low. Persistently high incentive earnings will suggest that it is low, but it will require a deeper examination to find the causes. The basic question to be addressed is: have incentive earnings been matched by higher output, better quality, speedier deliveries, or whatever it was the scheme was designed to achieve? If not, why not? The other questions which need to be posed by the team are: what assumptions were at the basis of the formula, and how do these assumptions now square with the facts, and what can be done to make the formula a better fit with the experience?

Perhaps less central but equally important, the team needs to look for any evidence that the scheme is inhibiting change, e.g. employees resisting moves or new technology where it would affect incentive earnings. Does the scheme make it harder or easier to reduce the numbers employed? Are employees refusing promotions which would take them outside the incentive scheme? Delving into these questions as well as looking at what effect the scheme has had on all costs, indirect labour, scrap, raw materials, utilities, maintenance, consumable as well as non-consumable stores items etc., is what the audit is for.

Many of the benefits which result from involving a wide span of employees in designing and introducing an incentive scheme, also apply at the review and monitoring stage. Supervisors, timekeepers, inspectors, accounts clerks, etc. may all have a perspective which enable them to make constructive comments on why the scheme is operating as it is, and how it might be improved. Similar techniques to those already described could also help to improve these contributions.

The Civil Service, which operates a performance-related pay system for senior civil servants, carried out an attitude survey in 1986 and discovered that although 75 per cent of the staff involved favoured the principle of performance-related pay, 68 per cent were opposed to the scheme in operation. As a result the scheme is being amended to accommodate some of the criticisms.

Hopefully the audit of the scheme will show that it is meeting its objectives, and merely requires some administrative adjustments. In some cases, however, it may uncover some major flaw which was not identified during the planning stages. If this is the situation the employer may then be forced to consider fundamental changes which might even require renegotiation. Almost invariably they will require at least more communication and perhaps some further training.

Chapter 8

What To Do If It Goes Wrong

8.01 Schemes which outlive their usefulness

Very few systems of payment last for ever. Organisations change. They expand or contract, move their geographical base, rationalise their structure, change the processes or technology, divert into different markets, develop new products or get rid of old ones, or perhaps the management philosophy changes when different people take over the business. Whatever the reasons, the circumstances which once made a particular payment system suitable alter, and sooner or later it is found that the system no longer meets the needs of the business.

Sometimes the changes which take place are only one factor, and employee or union pressures, or just inadequate management control, have led to distortion in what might otherwise be a suitable pay structure. All of these factors can be found when looking at incentive payment schemes which need updating or eliminating. Probably the most common reason for changing a pay structure which includes incentives is that the employer believes his payment method is not sufficiently cost-effective. This is often due to erosion of the scheme's criteria, leading to high pay for low performance standards.

A not uncommon situation arises when over the years improvements in machine tools, materials or product design are introduced without an adequate revision of the work standards, enabling employees to earn higher pay for the same or less effort. In non-manufacturing organisations, similar effects can occur when market conditions change, giving them advantages they did not previously enjoy, and without any increased effort by employees higher profits are earned creating bigger bonus payments. Similarly, if targets are not revised to reflect the effects of different prices, better products or reduced competition, salesmen can also earn higher commission with little or no extra work on their part. All payment schemes, therefore, need to be constantly examined to see whether they are still doing what they were designed to do, and to assess whether that is still what the organisation wants.

The motor industry provides examples of the need to relate pay systems to other developments. The two changes made to the Ford Motor Company's wages structure in 1967 and 1986 illustrate how they adapted to changing conditions. Ford, the only motor manufacturer in Britain that has never employed payment by results, had a simple wage structure that was the envy of the rest of the industry in the fifties and sixties. There were three wage grades, one for skilled, one for semi-skilled, and one for labourers, plus a management discretion merit system and well controlled conditions allowances which were confined to four job categories.

A national shortage of toolmakers led to the wages for that group falling below the market rate and pressures by them for additional pay. Simultaneously there was pressure from production workers to extend the conditions allowances. All this occurred in a period when shortages were creating recruitment and retention problems, particularly in the South East. The company decided that a piecemeal approach, especially in the labour relations climate at that time, would be too costly. With the aid of consultants they carried out a job evaluation exercise covering all manual occupations. When the existing wage structure was subjected to a detailed analysis it became clear that merit pay had been used to create a whole range of job rates around the three grade rates.

Following the job evaluation exercise, a five grade structure was negotiated and merit and conditions allowances eliminated. Because of their experience with the merit scheme, and because wages drift was rife in most other parts of the industry, a tightly controlled structure became a primary objective in the negotiations. Individual plants were given no discretion to alter grades which were determined by a central staff job evaluation team. By the 1980s, however, the lack of flexibility had become a serious inhibitor to change. The rationalisation of the manufacturing facilities to meet increasing competition led to the closure of non-economic plants, including the Foundry and Blast Furnace, and the increasing use of automation to replace traditional production jobs such as spraying and welding. Whereas, in 1967, management's concern was to get continuous output by maximum division of labour on short cycle work-studied operations, the new processes and technology and the need to eliminate over-manning and restrictive practices to survive against foreign competition required a better trained and more flexible workforce. This was achieved in the negotiations completed in early 1986 with a system of special payments, the effect of which was to eliminate most demarcations and reduce the numbers of indirect workers.

British Leyland, as it then was, had faced a different and more serious dilemma. Their incentive pay schemes had not only led to runaway labour costs (in some plants in 1969 workers were taking home up to 40 per cent more pay than their Ford counterparts), but were the cause of regular production losses because of disputes. Management's primary labour relations objectives were to move to a system of measured day work and replace the numerous wage bargaining groups with centralised negotiations. They achieved this after some well publicised struggles in the late seventies, and when they had sufficient control imposed a production bonus scheme in April 1980.

Vauxhall, who had abandoned a group bonus scheme in the 1950s in favour of measured day work, introduced plant-based production bonuses in 1978. This scheme was amended in subsequent negotiations, and in 1984 some of the bonus was consolidated and a new pay structure introduced. A combination of bonus payments and further consolidation depending on more flexible working etc. are now being used to reduce labour costs and increase output.

The Talbot-Peugeot organisation, previously Rootes and Chrysler, has employed systems of payment by results ranging from piece-work on machining operations to production bonuses, and now have bonuses linked to a Plant Performance Index (P.P.I). The basis of the index is standard hours *versus* actual hours it takes to build a car or produce components. They, too, have consolidated varying amounts of the bonus and increased the threshold since the scheme was first negotiated.

8.02 To adapt or abandon?

If an employer believes, and all the evidence points to, the pay structure no longer meeting the organisation's needs, then he has to decide what to do about it. One of the truest sayings in business is that, 'if you don't know where you are going, you are liable to end up somewhere else'. Put in the language of the business school this translates as 'without clear objectives and plans for reaching them, organisations are unlikely to stay on course and become successful and profitable'. So, faced with an ineffective incentive scheme, the employer needs to sit down and define what it is he wants his pay system to do before leaping in and making changes. Depending on the quality of his relationships with his employees and their representatives where these exist, he may well embark on a long consultative process or even a survey of employee attitudes before finally deciding on the change he needs to make.

Looking at the incentive scheme in isolation, however, will not enable him to define his aim, unless he is convinced that the non-incentive element of pay and his total personnel policies are fulfilling their objectives of enabling him to recruit, retain and motivate people, and that all he now needs is an incentive element to get that extra effort. If he has reached that conclusion then he is back to analysing his problem and defining the type of incentive scheme he wants, and how to change from the one he has. Alternatively, he may decide that he can best achieve his objectives without direct financial incentives, in which case he needs to decide how to get rid of the existing system.

Obviously the extent to which an incentive scheme is failing to meet its original objectives will be the determining factor when deciding whether to try and revive it or get rid of it. Only an analysis of the reasons for its failure will enable a sound decision to be made regarding its replacement. Even if it appears to be in a hopeless mess with little or no return for its cost this does not necessarily mean that a sound scheme could not be devised. A study may show that slack administration or poorly set standards are the causes of failure. In such a case the employer may be able to benefit from his experience and revise the standards or develop an alternative system of incentives which avoids the problems of the current one. If, on the other hand, due to changed circumstances the conditions no longer exist for a viable scheme, for example, because changes in process mean the employees cannot now determine the level of output, the employer is better to cut his losses and move to measured day work, or some other system of payment.

Unless the deterioration of the scheme has resulted in the employees not being able to earn any, or only very low, plus payments the employer has to recognise that change could be costly.

Put in simplistic terms, getting rid of an ineffective incentive scheme usually involves compensating employees for losing an easily earned element of their pay. The task facing the employer is doing that at minimum cost. How he sets about it will depend on a number of factors, the two most important being how big a proportion of total earnings is the incentive element, and whether or not the change has to be negotiated with the unions.

When buying out an employee benefit there are normally a number of options available which may enable the cost to be contained or spread over a longer period. Although every option should be considered by management, whether or not they have to negotiate the change, it may be decided to exclude some for tactical reasons when dealing with trade unions.

8.03 Buying the change

The first question the employer needs to consider is one of timing. Normally an employer who negotiates pay and fringe benefits will choose to negotiate out, amend or replace by another incentive scheme at the usual time he does his pay negotiations. Where pay is not subject to negotiations then he would probably choose the period when pay is normally reviewed. Many organisations carry out such reviews towards the end of the financial year when they know what funds will be available. If employee resistance to the change is anticipated because the opportunity of incentive earnings is being removed, then there clearly are advantages to being able to cushion the effect on employees with the usual annual increase or some other benefit.

Where this consideration does not apply either because the change will not result in any lost earnings opportunities, or because these are seen by employees as relatively unimportant, then the timing could be more flexible. Most managers believe it necessary to restrict changes to pay and benefits to one point each year. Those which are unionised do this partly to avoid facing pressures on economic issues on a continuous basis. These and others which are not unionised also see the advantages of predictable costs for planning purposes. One situation where an employer may choose to separate a change to his pay structure from normal negotiations or reviews is where he believes that the communication about the incentive scheme might suffer by confusion with other pay changes. He will be balancing the communication advantages against the ability to absorb some of his costs in the other items he negotiates or changes.

In the vast majority of circumstances it will pay an employer to introduce a change to, or eliminate, an incentive scheme at the time he is making other changes to pay and conditions. This will enable him to present the total changes in one picture in the most acceptable way. Where the change to an incentive scheme forms part of a long-term plan, he may well choose to coincide it with some other major change to conditions, such as an improvement to the pension plan, sick pay scheme, or reduction in the work week. Employees will then view the changes as a package, weighing gains and losses together. The employer needs to remember, however, that unless substantial, employees do not usually value fringe benefits as highly as wage or salary increases, and improvements which are most costly to the employer are not necessarily the most appreciated. The best example of the latter is work week reductions where the cost to some employers of replacing one hour's lost productive capacity can be high, but the employee will probably feel only little advantage. Similarly, a young workforce will not usually put improvements to the pension scheme above pay increases, irrespective of the cost to the organisation.

In considering the cost of change the employer needs to know which employees are going to be affected and by how much. If the incentive scheme provides different earnings for different individuals or groups, it is not sufficient to know just the highest and lowest or average for the whole company. Basing a negotiating plan on the assumption that a scheme can be bought out by adding the average bonus to the base wage or salary, for example, could prove a costly error, if the most influential group in the negotiations earn considerably more than that. Equally, it would be a waste of resources to compensate at the highest bonus level when in practice few employees ever achieve that.

The commonest method of compensation used when eliminating incentive schemes is consolidation, i.e. increasing base hourly, weekly or monthly wages and salaries by an amount equal to the average incentive pay. This is the most costly method because of the pyramiding effect; the resulting rates will usually become the new base on which shift and overtime pay, pensions, etc. are calculated. Where the consolidation involves only one section of the workforce it can also have the effect of pushing up the wages and salaries of the remainder as differentials are restored. All these new rates become the base for the next and subsequent increases. The experienced negotiator identifies in advance which elements of pay and benefit carry these additional costs, and tries to construct a settlement package with minimum pyramiding. One advantage of consolidation is that it can be used to boost to an acceptable level what might otherwise be seen as an unacceptable general increase. Where the amount to be consolidated is large it can, of course, be phased over a number of settlements if other circumstances make this feasible.

Combining both the points made above on the importance of knowing the target group and reducing on-going costs, can be achieved by a lump sum buy-out, red circling, or a combination of both.

As traditionally most employees have experienced little real security of earnings, inflation and the tax system have given few of them the opportunity to accumulate capital, and most have to live to the extent of their income, lump sums are attractive to the majority.

During pay bargaining trade union officials may put a long extended life value on a benefit, and attempt to draw the employer into negotiating on this basis, e.g. 'My members earn up to ten pounds a week from this scheme and, therefore, over the next ten years could expect without increases to get at least five thousand pounds'. The employer, however, does not need to respond on that same formula. His answer would probably embrace the fact that employees have no guaranteed level of incentive earnings, economic conditions make it impossible to predict one year ahead let alone ten years and the employees and unions need to look at their total pay and benefits package (including any improvements on offer). Depending on its credibility in the particular circumstances he could also refer to competitiveness and his labour costs, and what constitutes a viable cost base to provide some job security.

When preparing for and conducting any negotiations, the employer must do his utmost to reduce employee expectations. This applies particularly where lump sums are involved because these are unusual in transactions between employers and employees, and the latter have no reference points to curb the limits of rumour and speculation.

As with all changes to pay, whether negotiated or not, what counts in the end is their acceptability to the majority of employees. This means that judgements about employee aspirations, which have to be based on sound intelligence not guesswork, are as important as presentational skills at the table and communication skills afterwards. Like all such judgements it cannot be precise, but the sum eventually arrived at should prove significantly lower than one reached by any formula the unions would propose.

Red circling as a means of confining costs is a technique often used in buying out benefits or conditions in situations where not all employees suffer the same financial effects. The usual way of doing it, hence the name, is to separate out and treat the affected employees for a predetermined period as if the change was not being made. For example, if the employer wanted to abolish a merit scheme, all employees could be given an increase equal to the average merit and employees earning above that average would continue to have a sum equal to that extra merit paid on top of their wage or salary. Variations to this approach can be based just on time, e.g. the employees could enjoy this 'protected merit' for the remainder of their service or for five, ten years, etc. or qualified by future standard increases. In the latter instance the 'merit' may only be protected until it is absorbed by a future increase or increases. When combined with a lump sum buy-out a formula might be designed to give cash up front, instead of a pay increase, to compensate for the loss of merit up to the company average level with red circling of employees above that point. This approach is capable of considerable variation to suit the circumstances.

Before deciding which method to adopt the employer would need to calculate the relative costs of a range of options, taking into account not only the spread of merit payments but also the length of service pattern related to that spread. From this he could work out some cost projections based on levels of labour turnover. He would also need to calculate the calendarised cost of his options, not forgetting to weigh up the cash flow effects of a lump sum buy-out *versus* the on-going costs of red circling. Comparisons with the costs of consolidation including pyramiding should enable him to list and prioritise his options. Where he is going to have to negotiate the change this list will enable him to develop a negotiating plan with a range of bargaining steps.

In situations where one form of incentive plan is to be replaced by another, the available options increase. An approach adopted by a number of companies in recent years combines three elements, consolidation, revising the standard, and improving labour flexibility. In some cases these elements have been linked in a long-term agreement. Part of current average bonus or piecework earnings are consolidated and the threshold for earning bonus raised either in return for changes to working practices, or the working practices changes become the condition for later consolidation. In such deals time is added to money and productivity as a third variable, giving greater manoeuvrability in negotiation. An agreement involving these factors could, for example, take the following form:

Current scheme	*Year one*	*Year two*	*Year three*
Base rate plus bonus for performance over a standard 100 generating an average of £6 per week bonus.	£2 bonus consolidated in base rate and standard raise to 110.	Further £2 of bonus consolidated on condition that craft demarcations are reduced to minimum necessary for safe working and employees accept need to work flexible shift arrangement.	Further £2 of bonus consolidated, overtime cut by 50 per cent and threshold raised to 120.

Where the incentive scheme in operation has not been generating a reasonable level of bonus earnings, then pressures from employees for its removal or replacement will make management's task easier. Given these circumstances it should prove possible to adopt a joint problem-solving approach with the management's problems and objectives put to the unions or employees before the start of negotiations proper. These discussions might enable an alternative incentive plan to be worked out which avoids the problems of the previous one, or they may raise issues which could be best addressed by productivity bargaining.

Chapter 9

Productivity Bargaining

9.01 What is productivity bargaining?

A brief look at the available literature on the subject of productivity bargaining, which is not extensive, will show that the term can mean different things to different people. Some writers embrace all types of negotiated payments linked to productivity, including individual and group payment by results systems, and others confine their attention to specific types of collective agreements. Others see it as an exercise in employee participation. Because the purpose here is to consider productivity bargaining as an alternative to the types of incentive schemes already described, it is dealt with in the restricted sense of a negotiated deal in which employees accept changes in methods of working in return for improvements in pay or fringe benefits or shorter working hours, or some combination of these three. The essential differences between productivity bargaining and other forms of incentive are that productivity bargaining is about change, whereas most incentive schemes are designed to get employees to do more of the same thing. Also, the financial or other inducement to change is not usually a separately identifiable fluctuating payment.

Compared with piecework or group bonus schemes, productivity bargaining has a short history. The first two agreements which attracted any attention, one in the United States and one in Britain, were both concluded in 1960. Perhaps because the participants recognised they were embarking on something new they encouraged outside interest, and as a result both are well documented.

The American deal was negotiated in the West Coast longshore industry, or docks as we would call it in Britain. A powerful trade union had built up a crippling range of restrictive practices, not unlike the situation which existed in the London docks for many years. In the words of one union official: 'the employers bought the rule book'. They paid $29 million into a trust fund mainly to finance early retirements and lay-offs in return for the elimination of restrictive practices.

The British agreement, or agreements to be precise, were signed by the management and unions representing the manual workers at the Esso Refinery at Fawley, near Southampton. The employers paid increases averaging about 40 per cent in return for the relaxation of demarcations, the abolition of craftsmen's mates, more flexible shift working, etc. Some of the pay increase was to compensate for the loss of overtime earnings which were progressively reduced.

By the 1960s the British economy was beginning to feel the full effects of post-war developments, the loss of empire and all the trade advantages that went with it, the investment of national resources in a vast rehousing programme, the creation of a welfare state and, perhaps the most significant for industry, the emergence of strong competition from countries in Europe and the Far East whose industries had been rebuilt in the fifties. Labour costs which were considered high in Britain came under closer scrutiny. Although, in international terms, wages were not particularly high, productivity was low and successive governments both of the Left and Right saw the need to raise productivity. The sixties has also been described as a period of profit crisis for British industry. A succession of white papers on income policy stressed the need for pay increases to be related to productivity, and some stages of policy made a direct link by only permitting increases above a norm if they were tied to productivity improvements and were not passed on to the customer in increased prices.

As a result productivity bargaining boomed. At one stage the Department of Employment, which had a monitoring role, estimated it was examining eighty submissions a month. Although there were some notable exceptions, it is now generally acknowledged that many of these so-called productivity agreements were little more than devices to get around incomes policy restrictions, and that few resulted in significant and lasting improvements in productivity. It is the writer's opinion, however, that some managements gained useful experience in that period which enabled them to make real increases in productivity in later years.

9.02 When is productivity bargaining appropriate?

Most employers decide to embark on productivity bargaining when they have labour inefficiences such as demarcation problems, employees refusing to take on a wider range of tasks, resistance to moving from job to job or accepting shift work, or, in fact, any employee resistance to change that the employer needs and which he believes he can buy at an acceptable price. Employers adopting this method are usually seeking a quick, once-off but permanent, change in behaviour. Sometimes they recognise that they cannot solve their problem with a conventional incentive scheme as it does not include those elements which are essential for such schemes to work, or it does have the ingredients but they are apprehensive about the possible open-ended nature of costs in an on-going scheme, or concerned about the effect on differentials. They may see the buying of change by a productivity bargain as quicker and more containable than changing the pay structure by introducing payment by results, using that term in its usual sense. These can all be sound reasons for considering productivity bargaining, but there are also other factors which have to be present for this approach to be successful.

A proper problem analysis must be carried out to ensure that the employer fully understands the inefficiences he wants to eliminate, and the reasons for them. Many a productivity deal has failed because management has not probed deeply enough and assumes that problems which require some management action are solely due to employee or union attitudes. They may think, for example, that demarcation is entirely due to bloody-mindedness on the part of unions and employees, when in fact it stems from the way work has been organised or the rigidities of the wage structure. Other common mistakes are ignoring the role that supervisors play in the control and allocation of work, and believing that discipline can be negotiated with trade unions. In other words, before starting down the road of productivity bargaining the employer needs to be satisfied that the employees have it within their power to deliver the changes he intends to pay for. The following examples of inefficiencies and some possible causes illustrates this point.

Problems	*Possible causes*
Craft demarcations.	Organisation of maintenance/tooling/machinery/ inspection work. Differences in skill/training. Supervisors' attitudes. Wage structure.
Excessive overtime.	Lack of an effective overtime budgeting system. Authority for overtime too low or too loose. Ineffective control of work rate in standard hours. Low basic pay. Poor work organisation. Shop floor agreements on overtime allocation, e.g. 'one in all in' arrangements.
Late starts and early finishes.	Slack supervision. Insufficient or poorly sited time clocks. Inadequate catering service. Inadequate parking or transport facilities. Overmanning.
Resistance to technology change.	Ignorance. Fear of redundancy. Fear of skill inadequacy. Loss of incentive earnings. Concern about break-up of work groups. Health and safety concerns.
Resistance to shift work.	Lack of transport. Loss of overtime earnings. Inadequate shift premiums. Employees' domestic problems.

Problems	*Possible causes*
Resistance to the use of agency labour.	Fear that rates of pay will be cut. Fear that all that type of work will be given to agency with consequential redundancies. Fear that inexperienced agency staff will produce low quality work which will impact on performance and result in criticism of permanent employees.

These examples indicate the need to understand the real causes of problems and not jump to conclusions about employees' attitudes. A thorough anlaysis will probably indicate a range of actions that are needed, some of which may form part of a negotiated package and others not.

Although only referred to once above, and then only as a possible cause of demarcation, a wage structure can be a major inhibiting factor when trying to improve productivity. The potential problems in some incentive schemes which can create resistance to change have been referred to earlier, but other types of wage structure can produce similar results. Where systematic procedures exist for allocating jobs to wage or salary grades such as job evaluation, it is common for the process to include some form of job description. Even if only designed as a general guide these can easily become restrictive as employees will believe, perhaps understandably, that the job description describes what they are required to do in return for their pay, and that nothing more should be expected of them. Because wage structures so often act as inhibitors to change, frequently productivity deals involve changes to the method of payment as well. They do not have to go together but often do. Changing the structure invariably alters the pattern of differentials, and can make the negotiation of improved productivity more complex. Conversely, because a well thought out and executed productivity bargain should be self-financing, it would normally make the total level of pay increases more attractive and thereby facilitate the acceptance of changes to the structure. A need to change a wage structure and the costs involved might also make that an appropriate time to do productivity bargaining.

If the pressure to enter into productivity agreements in the sixties came primarily from incomes policies, the pressures in the eighties arose from the increasing competitive conditions exacerbated by the effects of inflation on production costs, and the effects of an oil-based currency on prices in export markets. With the drop in use of capacity caused by the recession of the early eighties, output-related incentive schemes lost much of their impact, and this also acted as a reason for some employers to look at other ways of increasing productivity at the same time as reducing costs. All organisations where labour formed a significant part of operating costs were forced to tackle over-manning. Depending on the nature of their business and their problems employers tended to tackle the situation in three ways: cutting the numbers employed by closures and redundancies, improving labour utilisation by getting rid of restrictive practices, and investment in new technology. Most used a combination of all three, and those that were unionised found themselves negotiating change but this time from a position of strength, as unions and employees saw only too clearly the stark alternatives facing them.

The eighties could be described as the decade in which British managements discovered what competition was really about, and unions and employees discovered that profits, productivity and costs really mattered to their jobs.

9.03 What can be bargained?

The short answer to the question 'What can be bargained?' is anything the employees can give and the employer is prepared to pay for. This again emphasises the importance of analysing the productivity problem, and making a clear separation between those things which it is in the employees' power to do and those where action is required from the management. In some instances some action from the union may also be required, for example where a particular restrictive practice stems from a union branch, district committee or executive ruling. These, however, are much rarer in practice than the public or even the employer is sometimes led to believe. Again, craft demarcations provide a good illustration. In a small firm employing one or two men on maintenance work, those men will probably do every repair that arises working in different materials, using a wide range of skills and often both making and fitting components. Their title will often be a general one such as maintenance fitter, or sometimes for vague historical reasons they might be called millwrights or some other name. If they leave that firm and are engaged by a large organisation employing many mechanical maintenance craftsmen, they will probably be allocated to a particular section and assume a title which goes with that section. They might be called machine repair fitters, or installation fitters, or factory services fitters. Probably their supervisor will be also called machine repair foreman, installation foreman, etc. Their skill, apprenticeship and union have not changed, but the management has decided to delineate responsibilities and custom and practice develop so that men only carry out certain work or work in certain areas. Within these management-arranged divisions group loyalties grow up, overtime is allocated, etc., and practices develop which create vested group interests. As a representative of his members' interests, the shop steward will guard the *status quo*. The trade union, in the form of district and national offices, will support the members, but unless some change is proposed which cuts across an industry-wide agreement or a basic union rule they will always be prepared to negotiate. With the devolution of power in most unions that has taken place in the past twenty-five years, officials will seldom attempt to resist any change that is acceptable to their members. Relaxations on demarcations which may be more strongly resisted are those which involve questions of safety or competence. This does not mean they are not negotiable, but usually indicate that some changes will require more than just money to effect.

The changes which have featured most frequently in productivity deals in the past are alterations in the pattern of hours, including the introduction of shift patterns and the reduction of overtime, job flexibility between different crafts, between craft and non-craft, between different types of non-craft, between shifts and departments (and, less frequently, between blue collar and white collar jobs), elimination of some job titles such as mates, new technology, work being contracted out and reduced manning levels.

Although productivity bargains involving manual workers are still more common, the number of deals covering white collar staff is increasing. The problems of measuring the productivity of salaried staff has, however, led most employers to use the crude method of simply setting headcount targets, and using extra pay as an inducement to make less people do the same or more work.

9.04 Preparing for productivity bargaining

There is an old army saying to the effect that time spent on reconnoitring is worth an extra battalion, and throughout this book the importance of thorough problem analysis and detailed planning have been repeatedly stressed. Productivity bargaining, like any other negotiation, requires careful preparation. Part of this process may involve educating management.

When the idea of productivity bargaining is first raised it will, in most cases, be in circumstances where there is no experience of the technique, and some managers will have totally unrealistic expectations of what is achievable. In particular, senior management, who seldom have current first-hand experience of shop floor problems, will sometimes believe, for example, that total flexibility within the workforce is both desirable and achievable. Or, and this also is not an uncommon belief, they will believe that the workforce will automatically become loyal and dedicated if only trade union influence can be removed. Conversely, managers may have accepted a low level of productivity for so long that they become cynical and apathetic and do not believe the situation can be changed. This is not uncommon where forms of buying out inefficiencies have been previously tried and proved unsuccessful. Therefore, often the first stage is diplomatically defining what are realistic objectives to be aimed at when beginning productivity bargaining.

A useful starting point is to ask line management to list all the practices, which may or may not be embodied in existing agreements, which they regard as preventing the achievement of higher productivity. Normally they will require help in this exercise because some problems will have existed for so long they will be regarded as intractable. Others may not be recognised as problems until alternative ways of doing things are pointed out. In some cases vested interests may make supervisors reluctant to highlight certain issues, but supervisory involvement at this stage is vital. It would be unfair to the vast majority of supervisors to say that they collude with subordinates on inefficient practices, but in situations where financial inducements are not available to him years of employee or union pressures usually result in the supervisor allowing practices which help him to gain employee co-operation. Many of these are unknown to middle and senior management and only come to light when there is a breakdown in working relationships such as occurs in a strike, or where pressures on labour costs put every aspect of labour utilisation under the microscope.

If everything that needs changing is to be brought out into the open and listed, the managers and supervisors will need reassurance as well as help. They must be reassured that they are not going to be criticised or penalised for having allowed practices to develop, and helped to see the alternatives that may be available. Ways of doing this which have worked in some organisations involve holding meetings with managers to explain the objectives of the enquiry and use this, and subsequent meetings in which supervisors are also included, to do basically three things. First to declare an amnesty and give a top management assurance that no one will be criticised for past and current practices that are revealed. Second, where fear is present as a factor, and it is never completely absent in any organisation irrespective of the management style, then it can be used in conjunction with the amnesty by making it clear that a serious view will be taken if it is subsequently discovered that the chance of tackling some inefficiency has been lost. Third, by getting people to share experiences and discuss problems they will get the confidence from knowing they are not unique and this will also encourage them to be more open. The whole exercise can also be structured as part of the process of getting commitment to change by including presentations on the state of the business, cost objectives, etc.

In some circumstances, confining the first and perhaps bigger meeting to the presentation and to the first two steps, and using smaller, perhaps departmental meetings for the third will be more appropriate. The choice may depend on whether in the particular organisation departments will become defensive and conceal from each other their inefficiencies or not. Where such problems exist more than usual effort may be needed to identify all the practices which have to be eliminated or changed.

It can be useful to have individuals or a working party sitting down with groups of managers and supervisors and compiling, or helping to compile, the list of problems. Personnel officers, providing they are sufficiently knowledgeable about day to day operations, can often play a valuable role, as can O & M or work study specialists. The list of known problems will slowly expand as new ones are identified and cross checked in other areas, revealing both duplication and variants. In checking on overtime costs, for example, it may be revealed that excessive hours in maintenance are due to the practice of 'one in, all in' – that is, particular trades refusing to work on overtime unless the whole of their trade works. In other words, a number of men may be paid at overtime rates for hours when the job requires fewer or even just one man to work. Following up enquiries about this practice in other departments may reveal variations such as production operators only agreeing to week-end work if the whole department including indirect employees also work, or safety and first aid staff are called in, or stores staff who will only receive incoming goods in overtime hours if fork-lift truck drivers and material checkers also work.

Although many productivity deals have aimed at reducing the level of overtime worked, others in industries where overtime is needed to meet production peaks have aimed to seek compliance with overtime requirements and/or to reduce the costs by ensuring that week-day overtime, when premiums are lower, is worked before high premium hours on Saturday and Sunday. A skilled personnel officer will be able to use examples of practices uncovered to probe and encourage the disclosure of similar or related practices elsewhere. Slowly, over a period of weeks, a dossier can be compiled describing all of the inefficiencies which could form the grounds of productivity bargaining. Before this is complete, however, the next step, costing, can start.

It will quickly become apparent that the degree of management emotion attached to a practice is not necessarily a good guide to its importance. Managers can become quite irate about issues which they believe involves management prerogative, even if the cost is negligible, and ignore other high cost issues which do not have the same implications. As management's prime responsibility is to reduce costs and optimise profits, effective managers will concentrate on the latter issues. Having compiled the list or dossier of inefficiencies, the cost benefit to the organisation of eliminating them needs to be calculated as quickly as possible. This cannot be done precisely but needs to be sufficiently accurate to enable assessments to be made of what the organisation should pay for the changes to be made. Although savings in materials, tools and overheads will result in many instances as improved efficiency improves quality, reduces scrap and increases facility utilisation by reducing equipment downtime, the biggest savings normally occur in labour costs. Unless everyone accepts, albeit reluctantly, that improved efficiency will probably mean less people then the task of effecting real improvements is going to be even more difficult. Pressing each area manager or supervisor for an estimate of what headcount saving can be made by resolving each inefficient practice identified is a necessary discipline. It can serve the added purpose of removing excuses from the less able manager who will be forced to agree he could do the job with less people, or admit that the practices are not a significant factor affecting the performance of his area.

A comprehensive cost evaluation, if the changes in work practices are significant, should include all the knock-on effects both positive and negative. A deal which resulted in employees producing work of a higher standard, rectifying errors and certifying it met those standards, could result in the drastic reduction or even elimination of a quality control function. A willingness on the part of direct workers to carry out running repairs combined with a breakdown of craft demarcations could decimate the maintenance department. The acceptance of computerised systems or other office technology could make an invoice processing department redundant overnight. Such structural changes will probably create savings at the supervisory and management levels, but will also usually involve the costs of making people redundant, or persuading them to accept early retirement terms. The cost savings that can be made by slimming down an organisation, some not even recognised at the time the decision is taken, are considerable and should more than justify the resources of time and skill devoted to planning and negotiating the changes.

With a comprehensive list of inefficiencies and an estimated cost alongside each, the employer has the basic data from which to start making some estimates and judgements. He can group the problems, decide on his priorities and estimate what he can afford to buy. This will, of course, also require some feel for how strongly employees will resist change on particular points. Armed with the evidence of possible savings, the employer should take steps to make sure the board and the whole management team are committed to their achievement.

The principles and steps described in Chapter 6 on communicating, negotiating and introducing financial incentives apply also to productivity bargaining, but with some variations. Management commitment to effecting change is absolutely critical, the bargaining process has to involve employees who will be part of the changes and managers who understand the detail of what is being negotiated, systems will have to be devised and agreed for ensuring change actually takes place after negotiation, and all the employees affected will have to know, understand and accept what will be required of them. All of this requires detailed pre-planning.

9.05 The machinery of negotiation

Although it is now customary to have lay representatives on negotiating bodies, frequently they are in the minority and play a watching and listening role. Where the matters under discussion are fairly simple such as straight pay increases, work-week reductions, or vacation improvements, the results can be easily conveyed to employees who will decide to accept or reject them. The role of the lay representatives is then largely confined to ensuring that the full-time union official, or officials, conducting the negotiations understands what is likely to be acceptable to the members and conveying to the employees the text and flavour of the meeting. In productivity bargaining, where the discussions frequently revolve around the way tasks are allocated and carried out, only employees who have the practical experience are equipped for such debate. The officials will understand the union policy and principles and some of the practice from their own experience and from the briefing of employee representatives, and play an active, if not leading part, in the discussions. They will, however, depend on the representatives for an understanding of the relevant custom and practice and employee attitudes. The employer, therefore, even if it is not suggested by the union side, will need to consider supplementing the customary bargaining machinery. If the normal process involves centralised bargaining covering a number of units, he can enlarge the negotiating committee or consider a two-tier negotiating arrangement, or divide the negotiations into separate sessions, some dealing with overall matters and others which deal with particular problems or particular locations. He could, for example, in conjunction with the unions, set up a series of joint working parties to handle different issues or the same issues in different locations, maintaining the normal committee as a co-ordinating body and to do the negotiations on the principles and items common to all such as money.

In any course which involved a number of bodies, the terms of reference of the subsidiary ones would need to be clearly spelled out. If, for example, the employer was willing to pay *x* per cent for the introduction of shift working for salaried engineers with the minimum requirement to qualify for the payment, at least 50 per cent of engineers on shift in each local unit, these limits would have to be made clear. The local working party or subcommittee then might discuss how the shifts would operate and how people would be allocated, but would not have the authority to negotiate the *x* per cent money or the 50 per cent requirement. Although in the circumstances of a multi-unit group which normally did centralised bargaining it might be felt useful to give autonomy for local bargaining on money as long as some broad overall budget was not exceeded, the dangers are that local units would go in different directions leaving practices untouched in some which had been bought out in others. This could set the scene for leap-frogging claims in the future. Where decentralised bargaining was usual group practice or only one unit exists the same problems might not arise, and all that will be required would be to ensure appropriate employee representation at the table.

Apart from the risks of divergence which can be overcome with the type of controls suggested, the main potential hazard to normally centralised bargaining from the two-tier method is that one unit may fail to reach agreement within the guidelines, and put the total deal in jeopardy. In such an event the employer will have to hold fast to the criteria, refusing to pay until all have complied, and rely on peer pressure to bring the recalcitrant unit into line.

Supplementing the employer's side of the bargaining team by including people with detailed knowledge of working practices is not difficult providing care is taken in the selection of individuals and ensuring they are properly briefed. This briefing should include not only an understanding of the employer's negotiating objectives, but also the exact contribution the individual is required to make to those negotiations. Inadequate briefing can lead to embarrassment, if not worse, if, for example, through ignorance at the joint meeting participants on the company side appear to be accepting lower standards of labour flexibility than the employer is aiming for.

In summary, negotiating arrangements which customarily only deal with broad issues of pay and conditions, and which comprise mainly senior company and union officials may not be suitable for productivity bargaining. If they are modified in one of the ways suggested, the modified machinery will probably require some controlling mechanisms.

9.06 Planning the implementation

One of the lessons managements have learned from experience is that statements of intent, or even words in an agreement, do not by themselves bring about changes in behaviour. Just as with the introduction of an individual or group bonus scheme, the employer has to think through and set up procedures if the efficiency changes are to operate from the start.

Although he will not know until the end of negotiations precisely what is agreed, the employer can draft plans based on reasonable assumptions. These plans will need to embrace communications to management, supervision and all affected employees, administrative arrangements linking pay to changes, training, redeployment and, possibly, redundancies. Just as with any other form of incentive the 'incentive to change payment' embodied in a productivity deal has to be related to the change in behaviour. The employee needs to recognise the relationship between what he is doing and what he is being paid.

If, as sometimes happens, there is a delay preventing every individual from carrying out different tasks immediately, he should still be able to see the evidence of change around him and clearly understand why he is not yet affected and when he will be.

The employer, therefore, needs to consider just what is required to force changes to happen and recognise the dangers of just hoping it will occur naturally. The following examples illustrate the type of action which can be planned in advance:

Acceptance of new technology: time delivery and installation of VDUs, numerically controlled machine tools or other automated equipment so that employees have to use it as soon as the deal is signed up.
Demarcation: instruct supervisor to allocate employees to work they are capable of doing but have previously refused to do.
Acceptance of shift work: notify employees of changes in working hours.

Undertaking training for new or expanded roles: set up training programmes and allocate employees a time and date to attend.
Overtime flexibility: draw up overtime rota which cuts across all previous restrictive overtime practices.

Planning such actions does not mean that the employer is insensitive to the need for proper consultation about change, which may have to be extended after the conclusion of negotiations, but these measures will quickly flush out whether employees and their representatives fully understand and accept what has been agreed, as well as enabling employees to relate their pay increase to changed practices. This proving out needs to occur before payments are actually made.

The very nature of productivity bargaining creates more detailed agreements than usually result from negotiations, and thereby requires an equal need for detailed communication. The agreement language may be broad and general, but somewhere, either in the minutes of meetings, or appendices to the agreement, the detail has to be captured. A general statement in the agreement to the effect that the unions accept the need for changes in working hours, including introduction of rotating shifts, will need amplification to be effective. If the minutes record that this gives the management the right to vary starting and finishing times, and introduce any pattern of shifts with ten working days' notice, and they propose to do that in X, Y and Z areas within the next six months, that needs communicating. Posting or distributing copies of the agreement will not be sufficient.

Normally different groups of employees will be required to accept different changes, so blanket communications on principles which do affect the whole workforce will have to be supplemented. Some changes, such as relaxation of demarcations, will have different effects on different groups, many of them small, and even on single individuals. This could be the case, for instance, in a maintenance or fabrication department where employees with specialist skills such as coppersmiths are employed. If one coppersmith is going to be employed on a wider range of work involving different materials, equipment, etc., or undertake training to acquire new skills, someone will have to tell him. That someone will have to understand the spirit as well as the letter of the agreement, or one set of demarcations could easily be exchanged for another.

The communication plan has to embrace everyone involved. Management, as well as all employees covered by the agreement, have to understand thoroughly what has been agreed, and how and when each change will be implemented. First-line supervisors will have an important part to play, both in communicating change and in seeing that it happens. It will be advantageous to have meetings with them, perhaps while negotiations are progressing, to identify in advance problems which could obstruct implementation. Such sessions often identify simple but important points, such as there not being enough welding kits available if in future fitters are going to do their own welding. Forseeing and planning for such eventualities will enable full and effective implementation of change to take place. Anything which slows down the introduction of change creates a risk that the change will not take place, or be resisted when it does.

If one of the aims of the productivity deal is to cut costs by reducing headcount, then how this is to be achieved should also form part of the implementation planning. Tempting though it may be to phase reductions over a long period relying as much as possible on volunteers and natural wastage, serious consideration must be given to how this will affect the degree and speed of change. Many inefficiencies arise from, and are encouraged by, overmanning and, conversely, a reduction in manning gives an impetus to more efficient working practices. If, therefore, the plan involves relying on volunteers and natural wastage, consideration should be given to redeploying people from areas where heads are to be cut. If some such steps are not taken then one of the most effective disciplines to accelerate change is missing. In retrospect this has been identified as one of the reasons why some earlier productivity deals failed, even where the willingness to change existed within the workforce. Put simply, as long as two people exist to do a job two, and not one, will do it, and if they have specialist skills they will continue to be used on jobs that best use those skills and not others.

Because redeploying people, especially within an organisation that is trying to make headcount reductions in all areas, is difficult, using redundancies or attractive terms that accelerate voluntary terminations is normally preferred. This will not usually provide a total answer to the need to reduce numbers quickly in the right places. The extent to which people volunteer is affected by factors such as age and alternative work opportunities, and even a compulsory redundancy is likely to be subject to some seniority rules, or other criteria. The plan may, therefore, need to encompass the facility to redeploy internally as well as methods of terminating employees. In a large organisation it is usually possible with ingenuity to create temporary work by stockpiling, refurbishing plant and premises, or by doing work usually put out to contract. Even if some on-cost is involved, if planned carefully as part of the process to accelerate change, it might be justified.

One aspect of planning the implementation which will be based almost entirely on assumptions about the result of the negotiations is the timing of the payments. Between the employer's objective of 'no money before delivery' and the union's objective of 'pay on the promise' some compromise is nearly always necessary to get the best fit around employees' willingness, the limits of training capacity, etc. Faced with this plans can still be drawn up, including the degree of individual commitment to be evidenced to qualify for payment. Just as in a multi-unit bargaining situation problems can arise with one unit holding out and refusing to comply, so with any productivity agreement individual employees or groups can refuse to adhere to the agreed changes after the agreement is signed. This contingency needs to be considered at the planning stage as the timing of other steps in the implementation process could hinge on it. The computerisation of payrolls, especially in large organisations, reduces some of the flexibility to make or stop payments at short notice that previously existed. These are the type of practical problems which differ from organisation to organisation.

9.07 Planning the negotiations

Again, all of the principles applicable to planning the negotiation of a financial incentive are relevant in planning productivity bargaining. The process of identifying and costing objectives, evaluating employee and union aspirations, and the criteria to be observed in selecting the negotiating team are referred to above, or in an earlier chapter. A similar type of format can also be drawn up listing the employer's objectives, the known union position, and compromises acceptable to management and itemised costs set out to provide a series of steps between 'offer' and final position.

An assessment of the union position will probably show that one of the first major obstacles to be overcome is that of job losses and, therefore, that has to be dealt with before any worthwhile dialogue on work practice takes place.

One well tried method of doing this is to start off the meeting with a detailed presentation of the organisation's financial position, using some of the techniques described earlier to make it interesting such as interspersing words and figures with pictures of products, processes, etc. This presentation should be designed so that, if the facts justify it, it culminates with the clear message that unless significant changes are made, competitiveness, profits and investment will suffer until big job losses are inevitable. In other words the aim should be to start off the negotiations from the base that the choice is not between standing still or accepting job losses, but making changes which will result in less people being employed or going downhill and facing massive, if not total, job losses.

Whenever possible, comparisons of practices and manning levels with more successful competitors should be used to give credibility to the message about the need for change. Where the numbers and cost involved will enable manpower reductions to be handled by voluntary redundancies and early retirements, an assurance given at the end of the presentation that there will be no compulsory redundancies might go a long way towards overcoming resistance. However, where strong employee opposition to any change is anticipated, it might be judged expedient to keep this 'give' until later when the unions can use it with their members as evidence of having negotiated some gains. Only an experienced negotiator with a full understanding of his own situation can make sound judgements on such points, as there are no general rules which apply on the timing of concessions. Except, the cynic might say, never make a concession unless it gains you negotiating mileage!

One fundamental decision that must be made at the planning stage is the form the payment for change will take. If the employer is satisfied with the pay structure that is in place, believing it to fulfill its main objectives, and it results in a generally acceptable pattern of differentials and causes no conflict, he will favour a method of paying for productivity improvements in a way which does not disturb this structure. He will, therefore, be seeking ways to give all employees approximately the same percentage increase.

A lesson that managements have learned from experience is that you cannot expect employees to give much in return for a pay increase that others are getting for nothing. Any system, therefore, which rewards everyone by an equal amount should seek some return from everyone, even though it may not be practical to get an equal change or sacrifice from every group or individual. To minimise resentment the changes effected should embrace all and individual contributions should be evident to other employees. If the identification of inefficiencies and negotiating objectives shows up gaps, i.e. groups or categories of employees not affected, then steps should be taken to include them. There are few situations where employee efficiency cannot be improved. If internal management discussions do not reveal the way to do it then a check on how other companies, including foreign ones, carry out similar tasks will normally reveal more efficient ways of doing things. The involvement of a cross section of management in this whole planning process will add to their commitment and contribute to the final success of the bargaining.

Even where the objective is to leave the current pattern of differentials intact there is still some freedom of choice in the way the payment for productivity is made. It can take the form of a straight percentage increase in hourly wage rates or annual salary, a lump sum paid once at the time changes are effected, a regular bonus paid weekly, monthly, quarterly or at some other frequency, or it can be paid in the form of an allowance which is added to the hourly rate or annual salary and paid with normal wages and salaries.

The factors determining the choice other than administrative convenience are usually the need to have a payment which employees can identify as a reward for their extra contribution, namely change, and which in size relates to the extent of the change. The employer may believe, for example, that a 3 per cent pay increase in hourly rates will not be seen as adequate reward for significant change, but if accumulated and paid as a monthly sum it will be. Payments expressed as an allowance, whatever the frequency of payment, with perhaps a suitable title, e.g. 'productivity allowance', enables the reasons for the payment to stay visible whereas increases in rates will get 'lost'.

Timing of change may be another consideration. If payment is being made for a significant change or changes which cannot be made immediately, management may decide that a lump sum paid out at the right time will have more effect. There are no rules which will apply in all circumstances, but the general principle that employees should see a link between what they do and what they get is as relevant in productivity bargaining as in individual or group incentive payment schemes.

In addition to planning the form the payment should take and the timing, consideration during the planning stage should also be given to whether or not payment should be withheld in circumstances when the qualifications are not being met. A distinction needs to be made between total non-compliance and individuals refusing to comply, and also the timing of such problems can be significant. A total refusal to comply or a refusal immediately following negotiations amounts to a failure to complete an agreement. This may be due to the negotiators misreading their degree of support, or communication failures. Whatever the reason, the solution must lie with the employees' negotiators, who have got to do whatever is necessary to get those they represent to accept what has been negotiated on their behalf. Although such a refusal may prompt the unions to seek changes in what they previously agreed, an employer would be most unwise to reopen negotiations on this basis. If pressed because the unions are unable to change the employees' position, the only practical response the employer can make is to take everything off the table, that is return to the situation that existed prior to the negotiations, making it clear to the unions that there is no more on offer and the productivity conditions for any pay increases remain the same.

Refusals by individuals or groups to comply immediately following the completion of negotiations also calls for action by the unions, probably with some help from the employer. In such circumstances the weight of the majority employee opinion can also be used, as they presumably will resent a minority delaying implementation of the deal. Once the agreement is operating then the terms are conditions of employment like any other, and a refusal by an employee or groups to comply should be dealt with like any other similar action. For example, a refusal to obey a management instruction, or carry out any aspect of normal duties would result in disciplinary action. The prudent manager would, of course, first ensure that the refusal was not due to a genuine misunderstanding of the terms of the agreement, seeking the union's help if appropriate.

Only if the unions were prepared to agree a clause providing for the withholding of a productivity payment, including a clear definition of how and when it should take effect, would it be sensible to operate such a policy.

Such contingencies need to be thought through so that advice to management on how incidents should be handled can form part of the training and communication plan.

9.08 Understanding attitudes in productivity bargaining

As stated previously in this chapter, the primary difference between negotiating a productivity deal and the more usual pay negotiations, is the amount of discussion of detail involved. The arguments in straight pay bargaining tend to revolve around comparability and cost of living with both sides using whatever figures best suit their argument. When productivity is brought in it is usually in general terms and only to bolster or belittle the claim. In productivity negotiations, however, once the principle has been accepted the arguments move from the general to the particular fairly quickly – from arguments about maintenance inefficiencies to why it is that an electrician cannot take off the panel to get access to an electrical circuit, or a fitter undo pipe couplings or use a sling and an overhead hoist. Discussions tend to move from that area to a debate about what skills people possess, what skills they can acquire through training, what happens to people who cannot absorb training or are made surplus, and how much the changes are worth. In the process many genuine and constructive points will be made, such as the need, and in some cases the statutory obligation, to employ properly trained people on certain jobs for safety reasons. Other arguments will amount to an emotional defence of craft traditions and job rights. While he might be dismissive of many of those, the employer needs to be sensitive to the strong beliefs held by men whose only marketable commodity is the skills they acquired in apprenticeship or at the technical college. As in all negotiations, patience is necessary to understand others' views so progress can be made by accommodating valid positions and effecting compromises.

An employer whose costs are pushed up by petty demarcations may require little more than an acceptance that craft employees use the skills common to all trades that are necessary to do the job in hand; agreeing that men will continue to be allocated on the same basis as before, e.g. electricians to jobs which are predominantly electrical, fitters to jobs predominantly mechanical, etc. but doing all the tasks needed to complete the job. Usually, however, he will be seeking more than that, wanting non-craft labour to do simple adjustments and repairs, and giving craftsmen broader skills so specialists such as welders and riggers can be eliminated.

Considerable improvements in efficiency can often be made without employees working any harder. People who have made a study of productivity in Britain and other countries frequently observe that British workers put as much, or more, effort into their work but do not work as effectively because of the way work is organised. Better organised effort can lead to more job satisfaction. A widened range of job responsibility can create more job variety and interest. Although it may not be politic to say as much in negotiation, the knowledge that this is the case can be helpful when trying to promote change.

Sometimes the employer's objectives can be met by the employees being willing to undertake duties that are well within their capabilities, and it is merely a question of buying their willingness. In other instances they will need to be trained to do more. Depending on the individuals and the circumstances, training can be welcomed or feared. People are proud of having being trained in something. Semi-skilled workers will often refer with pride to some programme of training they have received, even if it only lasted a few hours, recognising that it enhances their value to the organisation. As every trainer knows, training is a morale booster as well as a way of adding skills.

Conversely, employees can be apprehensive about training, concerned that they might not be able to absorb it and meet the standards set. Sometimes employees have not had to undertake any instruction since leaving school, which could be twenty or thirty years before. Resistance to training and other changes can sometimes be based on professional pride. Technically qualified and experienced draughtsmen may resent the suggestion that they should 'go back to school' before the introduction of CAD/CAM. Professional engineers may regard working on shifts as something more appropriate to manual workers and resist it as much as on those grounds as on its possible effects on their domestic life.

Appreciating the reasons behind resistance will enable the negotiators to articulate the organisation's needs in a less threatening way and carry this approach over into the communications. A misunderstanding of what the employer is seeking can, if conveyed to employees, jeopardise productivity discussions at an early stage. An employer who is sensitive to this will make sure his managers and supervisors can explain what is needed and quieten unnecessary fears, while at the same time not playing down the extent of the changes required.

The union's position in productivity bargaining is likely to reflect a complex mix of attitudes. The Transport and General Workers Union handbook *Plant Level Bargaining*, listing points for officials and representatives to consider, says the union's objectives in productivity bargaining are:

1. The more efficient methods progressively reduce the amount of effort required from workers in terms of work load, better conditions, shorter working hours, more satisfying work, and higher safety standards.
2. That the difference between capital and labour for the distribution of the benefits of increased productivity is clearly understood by all members.
3. That every agreement should involve an extension of negotiating rights and trade union controls and facilities.
4. That disputes procedure be such as to enable disagreements to be mutually settled without delay and in the workplace where they arise.
5. That the maximum weight is given to the social effects of changes before decisions are arrived at.

That may be a union's position, but the employee's concerns are more likely to centre around how productivity improvements affect his job security, how much and what sort of extra work he will be required to do, and how much extra money he will get in his packet or bank account. Some employees, because of their age or other ambitions may be contemplating retirement or redundancy with pleasure, and only concerned about the terms; others will be dreading the possibility of losing their job. Some others will be concerned about a drop in pay if overtime is cut, and others about the difficulties of providing company, or even protection, for their wives if they have to work night shifts. Some workers will welcome the relaxation of irksome restrictions; others worry about where their new responsibilities may start and finish. The experienced union negotiator will know that satisfying the diverse wishes of all his members is an impossible task, and will aim to get them maximum compensation for accepting changes or loss of jobs, and protection for those who may have difficulty in conforming to the employer's requirements. In reaching the best deal he can get the official will also be careful not to cross the line of accommodation to the point where he creates precedents which weaken the union's position in negotiation with other employers. Experience will teach him, as it teaches all negotiators, to compromise on the side of realism and that, for example, there is no point in fighting redundancies when many members are only too willing to accept the terms.

Some changes proposed by employers during productivity bargaining have more serious implications for unions than for their members employed in the bargaining unit. A reduction in the number of specialist trades could lead to the elimination of a number of small craft unions. The harmonisation of manual and salaried staff conditions can raise problems about representational rights leading to membership gains for some unions at the expense of others. The introduction of new technology can switch the emphasis in a workforce from unskilled to craft or *vice versa*. CAD/CAM can have major impacts on drawing offices, design studios and R & D staff, with consequential changes in union membership. Drastic workforce reductions leading to changes in organisation structure can often affect salaried staff more seriously than manual workers, and a staff union can lose its entire local membership almost overnight. All of these features can create union attitudes which although critical may never be mentioned during the productivity discussions by either side. Although the employer may be aware of these factors, and observe their influence on the negotiations, he is seldom in a position to mitigate these effects of change short of changing his own objectives.

One development in productivity bargaining during the recession of the nineteen eighties was the trading of work practice changes for some degree of job security. In essence the employer was saying: 'Unless you agree to change there will be factory closures and/or redundancies'. In some cases this developed from previous negotiations where job losses were involved, and the unions had adopted the stance that the price of more change had to be security for at least some employees. While most such negotiations were not recorded in this way, in some the understanding was formalised and assurances given that acceptance of new technology and more efficient working methods would not result in redundancies. Usually the assurance was qualified to mean no enforced redundancies and voluntary termination programmes continued.

In the United States where the combination of a recession and increased foreign competition had a similar impact on the manufacturing sector, agreements were reached in the vehicle industry which included provisions for retraining redundant workers. A college was established, jointly administered by the union and employer, and distance learning programmes were also organised. Some British employers such as the CEGB and ICI have also used imaginative approaches in dealing with people surpluses resulting from improved productivity. Whilst the small employer cannot involve himself in costly projects, he can often, at little cost, take steps such as collecting information of job vacancies and government training schemes and, delegating a member of staff to give advice, arrange interviews and help with letters of application, etc. Such proposals, if introduced into the productivity bargaining discussions, can, by signalling concern for the casualties of change, help to influence union and employee attitudes.

Another development in the recession of the eighties which could be interpreted as a form of productivity bargaining, although seldom described as such, was the negotiation of pay increases in excess of the rate of inflation in recognition of improvements in productivity. Improvements were largely facilitated by significant manpower reductions which unions accepted with only token protests. At one period these improvements in productivity combined with favourable movements in rates of exchange and led to significant reductions in British labour costs *vis-à-vis* overseas competitors.

These developments indicate a shift in attitudes about redundancies, early retirements and change where they are accompanied by acceptable levels of compensation.

9.09 White collar workers

Although the majority of productivity bargaining has involved manual workers, employers increasingly find they have to address problems of salaried staff efficiency. In manufacturing industry there was discernible progression in some companies, from first tackling overmanning in direct labour areas, to indirects and then salaried staff. In others, because craft restrictive practices were more obvious and received national publicity from notorious instances in shipbuilding, they were tackled before direct labour practices. Some of the resistance to management campaigns on inefficiency were due to their selective nature, and it often appeared that manual workers were being asked to take the lion's share of cuts.

There were, of course, understandable reasons why many employers took this approach. In smaller companies the salaried staff were often engaged, as the owner's duties outgrew his time, to do tasks he previously did. He had intimate knowledge of, as well as close day to day contact with, the work. Even in larger organisations senior management exercised a tighter control of salaried staff hirings, whereas the right to hire manual workers was often delegated to junior management. Manual workers, who frequently have less rights to security and enjoy less costly fringe benefits, are more likely to be regarded as expendable.

Another reason for the emphasis on manual workers' productivity is that in most organisations it is more easily measurable. This also largely accounts for the preponderance of effort related to incentive schemes in the manual sector.

Probably the two main pressures to tackle salaried staff productivity have come from rising salary and fringe benefit costs and office technology. Some earlier phases of office technology have, by creating factory-like conditions, made similar payment by results systems appropriate. Lines of punch card operators in one large office are not dissimilar from a workshop full of machinists on repetitive production work. A major insurance company was among the first to pay a bonus to data processing staff based on the number of key depressions per hour above an average.

Productivity bargaining covering salaried staff in manufacturing industries has been aimed primarily at two problems, resistance to new technology and the need to have all employees working compatible hours with some overlap in duties. The use of computers in all areas of business from design to material control and payroll administration, has replaced forms and drawings with VDUs and typewriters with processors. Slimmed down organisations, particularly if working to computerised systems, call for closer collaboration between all functions and levels.

This creates a need to reduce to the minimum differences in working hours and shift patterns. In some companies the changes negotiated extended to vacation policy, and the common practice of staff taking annual vacations at times to suit them curtailed to ensure adequate staff support throughout the year.

In organisations employing manual workers and salaried staff, and where both groups are represented by different unions, productivity bargaining becomes more difficult, especially if the employer needs to achieve an overlap or exchange of tasks between the two. Where internal relationships between the unions are good, then some progress is normally possible and can often be better achieved in bargaining sessions where all parties are represented. Merging manual and staff negotiating bodies, however, can also accelerate demands for harmonised conditions.

Although getting rid of the differences between salaried staff and manual workers might prove necessary to achieve the required level of flexibility, it might be too costly or pose other problems the employer is unwilling to face. Some organisations have traded staff conditions for improved working practices, taking the view that by adopting the initiative they can profit from what many believe is in any case an inevitable development. Many supporters of productivity bargaining will argue that its great attraction is its flexibility, and that the employer is only limited by his imagination and the money he has available to buy change.

Well planned and executed productivity bargaining is more likely to achieve sustained and worthwhile change if it reflects and produces changes in attitudes. Because employee attitudes and behaviour are a product of the totality of their working environment, worthwhile results, just as with other financial incentives, are also more likely to result if the bargaining forms part of an overall personnel strategy.

Chapter 10

Pay Strategy

10.01 Where is the organisation going?

There are very few organisations that have not felt the effects of change in recent years, and which do not predict even more changes to come. World-wide pressures on oil prices and rates of exchange, the effects of inflation on material and labour costs and interest rates, and changing technology are continuing to affect most employers and employees. There is also mounting evidence that the successful organisations are those that try to predict change, making the best forecasts they can and plan ahead to enable them to adapt more easily to a new environment.

The reasons are almost too obvious to need stating. Moving out of old markets and into new, changing pricing policy, developing new products and processes, introducing new technology and recruiting and training people to operate and maintain it, closing down plants or offices and starting up new ones, re-organising sales and distribution networks, computerising processes and systems all require long lead times and planning. The old breed of manager who prided himself on his adaptability and seat-of-the-pants approach is being replaced by the professional who uses sophisticated techniques for gathering information, analysis and planning strategies to accommodate change – looking for ways in which change can be turned into opportunity rather than a problem. Developing a strategy, therefore, is clearly an inseparable part of the top executive's responsibility for safeguarding the interests of shareholders and employees. It is within this overall strategy, the broad framework of long range objectives, that more detailed plans covering the short and medium term are designed and implemented.

10.02 The process

Put simplistically, the process for developing a corporate strategy consists of three steps or stages: an evaluation of where the organisation currently stands, an assessment of where it wants to be in the future, and a plan for getting from here to there.

The first step would include an evaluation or audit of the organisation, its performance and that of its main competitors or others engaged in a similar field, and an understanding of all the factors which make for success. The second step, perhaps the most difficult, is forecasting the conditions in which the organisation is likely to be operating in the future and setting broad objectives. Identifying trends, predicting developments, including what competitors are doing, is not all crystal ball work. Hard evidence exists on the size and structure of the population, for example, and if you are making or selling a product for the teenage market you do not have to guess how many sixteen-year-olds there will be in fifteen years' time. Changes in consumer spending habits are well documented and, for example, the shift from the use of public transport to private car ownership has been measurable for years. In most well run organisations much of this information will already be known or readily available, but some, such as likely technical developments, will need to be researched. Some factors, such as changes in legislation or political climate, will be a question of informed judgement. Again the emphasis is on informed, because even voting figures show trends and will probably provide a better guide to the future than a chat with the local MP.

From this mass of evidence it should be possible to create a picture or vision of what the organisation should ideally look like in ten, fifteen or twenty years' time – the customers it will be serving, the technology and materials it will be using, the skills it will need, etc. Changes in demand and technology, for example, might indicate that the organisation needs to change its structure, relocate, slim down the workforce, reduce its range of products or services, and use more automation. Alternatively, forecasts might suggest the need for a more decentralised organisation, or increased competition and investment in new products which the company cannot afford, and which calls for a strategy which includes withdrawing from manufacturing and concentrating resources on servicing customers.

When the appropriate corporate objectives have been identified, then step three, a strategy for moving towards this future 'vision', can be set down, the obstacles to be overcome described and a timing programme agreed. From this strategic plan the detailed plans setting down what needs to be achieved in the short and medium term can be drawn up.

10.03 Personnel strategy

Because organisations do not exist to employ people, but people are employed to enable organisations to meet their objectives, it follows that personnel strategies have to be designed with that in mind. In other words, they do not exist in isolation but should form an integral part of the corporate strategy. Similarly, because pay is only a part, albeit an important part, of an organisation's personnel philosophy and policy, it has to be seen as one component in an overall people strategy.

The steps involved in developing a personnel, or people, strategy will be basically the same as described above. In assessing the current situation it will be necessary first to take stock of the national scene – the labour supply, its geographical dispersion and degree of mobility, supplies of different types of skill and education and training for skill. The shift from the manufacturing to service jobs, from unionised to non-unionised, the increasing number of part-time and 'female jobs' are all relevant. The political and economic climate and legislative framework are also part of the national scene which can affect personnel policies.

Taking stock of the organisation's personnel position would probably start with an audit of its total human resources. A detailed breakdown covering everyone employed should include age structure, skills, absence and turnover data, and all in sufficient detail to predict shortages or surpluses at each and every level. This comprehensive approach is important as it would be pointless to have data which enables one to predict a shortage of software technicians or cost clerks, but does not show that three out of five senior managers reach retirement age at the same time.

The way in which the human resources are deployed, i.e. the organisation structure, as well as the way they are recruited, trained, motivated, compensated and 'serviced' are also essential parts of such an audit. This will involve an evaluation of all existing personnel policies, practices and procedures: for example, current recruitment sources and methods, selection procedures, training techniques, management development systems, and communication media. The modern personnel specialist knows that the cost-effectiveness of his function must also be subject to scrutiny, and will keep this in mind in doing the evaluation.

Last, but not least, the personnel audit will need to include updated labour costs and productivity figures. Where efficient costing methods operate and where there are established work standards, it is possible to produce reasonably accurate hourly labour costs. An hourly, weekly or monthly cost per person employed can otherwise be arrived at by adding together all the costs of employing the workforce and dividing it by the number employed. This sounds obvious, but the majority of organisations still ignore some of the costs involved. The three main components to be covered are wages or salaries, state fringes and other fringes. The latter should include pensions, sick pay, canteen subsidies, vacation and statutory holidays, and long service awards. Some companies include overtime and shift pay as a fringe, others as part of the wage or salary. It does not matter as long as they are included. When counting total employment costs as, for example, when comparing the cost of a large versus a small organisation, a share of the overhead to cover space, heating and lighting should be added.

Labour productivity is always difficult to measure, although direct labour productivity can be measured with reasonable accuracy where work standards based on well tried and expertly applied work measurement techniques have been established. Comparing labour productivity with other organisations or other countries, however, is a complex and time-consuming task which few organisations have attempted. The wide range of factors which can affect labour productivity ranging from tool and product design to calibre of management, make most generalisations on the subject, even if supported by 'nationally' produced figures, highly suspect and of doubtful value as a guide to action required.

This audit stage of developing a personnel strategy can be carried through without reference to corporate strategy, because it is only a study of what is. To move from there to a plan for the future requires a clear understanding of where the organisation as a whole is going. For illustrative purposes let us assume that intense competition from domestic and foreign companies requires a business to slim down the workforce, increase the use of automation and make substantial reductions in its operating costs, which it proposes to do by cutting salaried staff and devolving authority down the management chain. Part of the strategy also involves withdrawing from less profitable parts of the market, closing facilities which are only marginally profitable, and reacting faster to changes in demand even where that requires investment in facilities to produce products with a short market life.

Armed with this information, the personnel specialist can now create his own 'vision' of what the organisation of the future will be like in human resource terms. He can compare that with the picture produced by his audit, identify the barriers to change, and develop a strategy embracing all the people implications. This, which will include the pay strategy, will emerge, therefore, from the needs of the business. Prepared in the form of a report from the Personnel Director to the Board a description of personnel strategy for this mythical company could read as follows:

Strictly confidential
Copy 1 of 10.

ABC Manufacturing Group PLC. Ten year strategy for management of human resources.

Introduction

The corporate strategy agreed by the Board at the Norwich Conference in May requires for its successful fulfilment, significant changes in the company's total workforce and the introduction and continuation of a number of separate but related policies, some of which call for substantial investment. The following describes the current situation, sets out the objectives and identifies a number of problems and proposes solutions.

Current personnel status

Composition of the workforce:

The company employs 7,846 people full-time. Of these 86 as directors or senior managers, 260 as middle and junior management, and 480 as technical, clerical and administrative staff. The remainder are manual workers, approximately one-third skilled and two-thirds semi-skilled. The majority of the semi-skilled are women. The average age is 44 and 9 months and the average length of service is fourteen years for staff and eight years for manual workers. Of the total workforce, nearly 5,000 are employed at the Norwich and Kings Lynn factories, and the remainder at the four small plants and the stores depot. A detailed breakdown by location, age, skill category, length of service and wage and salary grade is contained in the appendix to this report.

Pay Structure:

The company applies common wages and conditions to all manual workers, and these are negotiated with three trade unions. Pay and conditions for salaried staff are reviewed annually at the same time as wages are negotiated, but are not subject to negotiation. With the exception of the profit-related bonus and share option scheme for main board directors no system of incentive pay is in operation. (Employees in the depot acquired in 1985 were on payment by results until then, when their bonus element was bought out and they were taken into the company pay structure.) The company, although not a member of the employers' federation, has used their local rates as a guide when recruiting. Our labour costs, which account for 54 per cent of our unit costs, have risen by approximately 6 per cent per annum for the past three years, which includes the cost of the improved pension scheme introduced during this period. Sick pay costs have increased with the rise in certified sickness absence referred to below. Although detailed information is impossible to obtain we believe our main competitors have absorbed wage increases by higher productivity, and have not suffered the same level of increase in their labour costs. A further cause of concern is that historically a paternalistic approach has led to an upward drift in fringe benefit costs.

Recruitment and promotion:

The company has traditionally relied on 'word of mouth' supplemented in some cases by local press advertising to recruit manual workers and junior salaried staff. Most supervisory and management positions have been filled by internal promotions based on the nomination of candidates by heads of departments. Senior management posts have been filled by the responsible director identifying people and recommending them for board approval.

Difficulties have been experienced in recent years in recruiting good electricians and computer staff, and there has been some criticism of the calibre of supervision and middle managers. Turnover of manual employees averages 15 per cent per annum and salaried employees 6 per cent per annum.

Training:

In the past five years a total of 23 apprentices have been trained, 3 newly appointed supervisors completed appropriate courses at a local technical college, and one manager, on his own initiative but with company support, attended a three month course at the London Business School. The Y.T.S. programme has produced 16 junior production operators.

Management development:

The performance appraisal system introduced at the beginning of this year has enabled us to identify three potential replacements for the seventeen departmental heads positions, eleven employees who with training should reach middle management, and two managers who appear to have senior management potential.

Absenteeism:

Unauthorised absence averages 1 per cent and sickness absence 7 per cent. Although this reached 11 per cent last February this compares favourably with other employers' experience. The 7 per cent, however, is 1 per cent up on last year and 2 per cent up on the previous year. Unauthorised absence is under 2 per cent, the majority of this being absence with permission for female employees.

Employee relations:

There have been no significant labour disputes since the pay strike two years ago, and the one day strike in transport over the dismissal of a driver just prior to that. Supervisors report that the new works paper is well received, and following the managing director's presentation in the canteen there has been much shopfloor and office speculation about increasing competition and its possible effects on the workforce. (Shop stewards are reported as saying they will call a strike if redundancies are proposed.)

Summary:

The company's workforce has remained basically the same in its size, structure and organisation since the company was formed in 1938. Relationships are stable, and the workforce appears loyal and reasonably well motivated, although they and the management have experienced little change to test those characteristics. It can be said that the total workforce is operating well but in a fairly comfortable rut.

Objectives:

To achieve the corporate objectives it would appear that the established workforce of over 7,000 people operating in a stable and fairly rigid organisation structure, producing products of constant design by traditional methods with largely semi-skilled labour in a total of six locations, will, over the course of the next ten years, have to be transformed. This transformation will involve the following:

Numbers employed:

Reduce the overall numbers employed from 7,800 to 4,500. To be achieved by closing the four small plants (2,300 employees), offering special early retirements to all employees over the age of 55 (700) and a redundancy programme for the remainder. Further actions to reduce headcount are dealt with below under the heading 'Organisation'.

Skills employed:

To operate and maintain the new technology it is estimated that two-thirds of the remaining or new manual labour force will need to be skilled. This will be achieved by retraining existing skilled employees, increasing the level of apprentice training to an annual intake of 20, using technical schools for the first year of training for each batch, training selected semi-skilled workers for skilled operator jobs. Supervisory training will be compulsory for all newly appointed supervisors and existing supervisors, who are not retired or made redundant, will be given short courses to meet individual needs as well as intensive training in the new technology. As our audit showed a serious shortage of professionally qualified engineers, and a low level of professional qualifications in all management grades, this will be addressed in future by recruitment actions and individually tailored as well as general management training programmes. The recruitment of graduate trainees, albeit on a small scale, will start next year.

To support this change to a better qualified workforce we have hired a consultant who specialises in selection. We believe he will recommend replacing the existing system of nominations and interviews with more sophisticated techniques, such as tests and assessment centres. He is also advising us on ways to improve the performance appraisal system, including ways in which it could eventually be extended to the whole workforce.

Management development:

The long established policy of promotion from within will clearly not be capable of meeting the company's needs in the next few years. In addition to the management training and graduate recruitment referred to, it is proposed that some external recruitment action be taken, particularly in those functions where there are no identified replacements for Departmental Heads and Deputy positions. To support this, and in the short term, it is proposed that one afternoon be set aside each month in the next quarter for the board to carry out a management appraisal and development review for the whole company.

Pay and conditions:

The current levels of pay will not enable the company to recruit and retain the types of skill it will need in the future, and the current structure tends to encourage long service and little else. To hire, retain and motivate the workforce, both those to be recruited and existing employees who will have to accept considerable change, in some cases acquiring new skills and responsibilities, the existing pay policy should be changed to one based on the principle of performance-related pay. Details of a bonus scheme based on company-wide performance but with a formula which encourages the shedding of labour will be submitted to the next meeting of this board. This principle will also be extended into this year's wage negotiations when, as previously discussed, a system of allowances in return for more flexible working will form the main part of the settlement.

As the company's future operating patterns, as well as the new technology, will require a more flexible workforce, it is proposed that this system of allowances be maintained and extended over the next five years, and concurrently the fringe benefits gap between manual and salaried employees be closed. The aim would be to move to a 'single status' workforce within six to seven years with the minimum of barriers to job flexibility. The single status pay structure would be based on two principles, a continuation of 'performance related' and the system of pay and fringe benefits being common from director to labourer with different levels of privileges, such as length of vacation, being related to service or responsibility level, or a combination of the two. Job descriptions, most of which are in any case outdated, would be dispensed with and replaced with position specifications used for organisation planning and recruitment purposes only. Separate plans to merge manual and staff catering facilities, and rationalise car parking and other privileges are in course of preparation. In the longer term, i.e. as a stage to follow single status, it is proposed to move away from annual salary reviews linked to annual performance appraisal in favour of a calendarised spread of individual performance-linked payments. The overall aim would be to create less standardisation and a more individual reward system for all employees.

Even though this strategy is planned to be implemented on a step-by-step approach, trade union resistance is inevitable due to the labour cut-backs, their eventual loss of influence when a significant part of the employees' reward becomes not subject to negotiation, and because single status usually involves the loss of membership from one union, or group of unions, to another. Negotiating plans will be drawn up which ensure that the discussions of pay structure changes do not coincide with discussions of redundancies.

With the planned decentralisation of management authority, a wider spread of managers will have the ability to influence profits. Although this is not proposed for the immediate future, the extension of the profit-related bonus and share option schemes to more managers should be considered. Extending some form of share scheme to all employees is not proposed until the results of the employee involvement actions recommend below can be assessed.

Organisation:

The current organisation structure and management style with which it is combined, leads employees, including managers, to identify with their function rather than the objectives and performance of the company as a whole. In addition, the chain of command, particularly, in the production departments, the biggest employers of people, inhibits good communication and firm direction, and encourages duplication of effort and record-keeping. The aim is to reduce the levels and produce a 'flatter' structure. As an intermediate step we should establish a system of multi-functional committees with responsibility for the specific actions needed to implement the 'Norwich' strategy, and chaired by departmental heads reporting to a co-ordinating group of executive directors.

Unless additional action is taken the planned headcount cuts will result in a reduction at the lower levels and leave an imbalance, i.e. too many chiefs for the number of Indians. It is proposed, therefore, that each function's headcount budget task require percentage reductions in each salary grade band. Initially this will be achievable by cutting out fat, extending managers' and supervisors' areas of responsibility, etc. The point should be reached within two years, however, where headcount budgets can only be achieved by structural change, by which time we will have closed the small plants, completed the major part of the early retirement and redundancy programme, and have a clear idea of the minimum structure needed to run the business.

Employee relations:

During the past forty years the company's relationship with its employees have become institutionalised. Little dialogue or communication takes place except through the medium of the trade unions. Salaried employees seldom have contact with any member of management except their immediate superior.

The MD's presentation, the first face-to-face meeting ever held between board members and the bulk of the workforce, was successful, but the tenor of the questions demonstrated little employee understanding of the company's problems and objectives.

The trade unions will react strongly to the proposals to close the small plants and reduce the workforce, but providing details of the generous separation terms are quickly made known they are unlikely to get much support from employees. Experience of other companies who have made these types of changes show that resistance can be overcome with the right level of compensation. The main objections will come from the general workers' union, who will recognise that the changes favour skilled workers. Our objective over the next few years will be to move to a smaller, highly skilled and flexible workforce, motivated by good pay and conditions and the knowledge that they are professionally managed. It is proposed that we adopt a more open management style, underpinned by a direct system of almost continuous communication of company plans and problems. This will take time to achieve as the majority of managers have been used to a different and more secretive approach to information 'sharing'. A separate paper dealing with communication policy and detailed proposals for improving communication methods is being prepared.

The change to a predominantly skilled workforce, improvements in conditions, particularly the move to single status and performance related pay, will reduce and confine the influence of the trade unions, and open the way for more innovation in the future.

For the purpose of keeping control of wage costs during the transition stage and subsequently, no change in the collective bargaining arrangements are proposed. Part of the process of 'opening up' our management style will be actions to involve employees more in problem-solving at every level. This tapping into a wider range of knowledge and experience, especially if reinforced by better communication, should raise the quality of decision-making, particularly in those areas where weaknesses in management calibre have been identified. If properly managed, such involvement should increase commitment and smooth the change process.

Resources:

It is obvious that we do not possess all the skills in-house for translating all of our plans into action. Although the closing of the small plants will generate some free managers who will provide good back-up support we will need to use outside resources (management consultants). A draft task specification for, and cost estimates of, these resources are being prepared for next week's special board meeting.

Conclusion

The major changes in the size, structure and philosophy of the company embodied in the corporate strategy agreed at Norwich require equally major changes in the management of human resources. The personnel strategy described above contains the ingredients needed to do this successfully.

Although dealing with a hypothetical situation, this 'report' illustrates how a personnel strategy might be designed to meet the needs of an organisation facing some significant changes.

Many organisations believe that to remain competitive they must develop leaner and more flexible workforces with barriers of organisation, pay and status reduced to a minimum, and within an environment where employees can be trained in and exercise a wide range of skills. It is far easier to create barriers to flexibility with pay than to remove them, and the sensible manager will be aiming to plan a pay policy that aids change and does not inhibit it. It is also useful to have a long-term vision of the type of pay structure one would like to see in place. Although this ideal may never be achieved, it provides a backcloth against which to plan shorter term changes.

It may be, of course, that a personnel strategy needs to be developed because it is believed that previous policies etc., are not meeting the organisation's needs, even though the organisation itself is continuing on much the same lines. Personnel policies often reflect the views of the man at the top, and a change of personality can require a new approach and a strategy to achieve it.

Probably the two main reasons for organisations re-appraising their personnel and pay strategies in recent years, however, have been cost pressures because of increased competition, and the declining influence of trade unions.

Cost pressures have caused many companies to consider their whole employment policy. Organisations with high wage and fringe benefit costs have recognised the advantages of contracting out jobs, starting with cleaning, security and catering, and then extending the practice to include maintenance, transport, etc., until only the core production or service is carried out by their own employees. The availability of inexpensive computers has also enabled some companies to use ex-employees, working in their own homes, on a contracted service basis. Temporary shortages of particular skills which push up their market price can prompt employers to hire these as an agency service, rather than distort their own salary structures. Using people on a contract basis can give an employer cheaper and more flexible resources, and enable him to provide greater job security for his own employees. Similar results can sometimes be achieved using casual labour.

Although Britain still has the highest proportion of union members of any Western industrialised country, the changes in the economy already referred to, namely the shift of jobs away from manufacturing and into the service sector, means that more and more employers are dealing with non-unionised workforces, or a situation where the union has only limited support. This enables the employer to experiment with ways of compensating and motivating employees with greater freedom than he would have if all changes had to be negotiated. In the United States, where a combination of circumstances similar to those existing in Britain has led many companies to start up or expand in areas where State laws make it easier to avoid unionisation, differences in personnel strategies are evident between them and companies in the unionised sector. Unfortunately, this has led to a belief in some trade union quarters both here and in the United States that some of the innovative concepts, including employee involvement, are anti-union in their intent. In both countries, decrease in union influence in the economy as a whole is leading to a move away from automatic externally driven pay increases, and towards individual performance-related packages.

The type of personnel strategy adopted, because it must be a part of a total strategy and serve the needs of the business, will be influenced by the technology and other factors which determine the levels of skills required. A company in the hi-tech sector will probably have as a primary objective attracting and keeping people with a high level of skill capable of inventing and developing new ideas. To achieve this it would probably be prepared to adopt policies and practices which the manager of a large Midlands foundry, for example, would find unnecessary and too costly.

Another effect of changing technology which may have a bearing on pay strategy is the way it increases or decreases labour cost as a proportion of unit or total costs. Improvements in technology usually result in an organisation becoming more capital- and less labour-intensive. If this change occurs as a result of numerous minor developments in technology over a long period, the shift in cost emphasis can go unnoticed by management, who continue to support a pay strategy linked to outdated principles.

Sometimes changes in technology, process, or even products, will affect the way work is organised. Apart from the implications for any incentive pay scheme this too can create the need for a different type of pay strategy, as the emphasis moves from the individual's contribution to that of a bigger work group. Alongside the trend towards performance-related pay for managers in particular, is another trend, not unrelated, pushing management decision-making closer to the customer, leading to a lower, broader based pyramid structure. A personnel strategy that does not also embrace organisational development may, therefore, miss factors critical for producing a valid pay strategy.

Few aspects of pay policy have caused as much debate as the arguments about centralised *versus* decentralised bargaining. To many employers the debate is of academic interest only, as their own needs, history, agreements or other circumstances lock them to the system they have. Some of the changes referred to, however, or the opportunities presented by green field site investments, enable employers to make a positive choice. Normally the choice is between the degree of control possible with one centrally negotiated set of pay and conditions, and the labour costs savings that can be made by taking advantage of regional variations in rates of pay. Again a business where labour costs form a significant proportion of total costs will stand to gain more from decentralised bargaining if other factors also make it viable. Understanding whether future changes in one's business are likely to result in the bulk of the workforce being employed in low cost or high cost regions, therefore, can also be important in determining this aspect of pay strategy.

It is obvious, therefore, that there is a whole range of considerations which have to be taken into account, and there is no one perfect pay strategy that fits all organisations. A pay strategy has to be an integral part of an overall personnel strategy, which in turn must be designed to fit the objectives of a corporate strategy. Without such strategies an organisation will be reactive and not proactive, and constantly running just to keep up with the changing business, political and economic environment. A management that allows this to happen is failing in its basic responsibility of making the most cost-effective and profitable use of the organisation's resources.

Because few employees have the luxury of operating in a static environment, strategies have to be regularly reviewed in the light of changing circumstances. This includes an organisation's pay strategy. Although frequent change in pay structures or methods is undesirable for all the reasons set out at the beginning of this book, it is important to ensure that significant changes in corporate strategy are reflected in the way it manages employees. A dynamic approach on pay will ensure that financial incentives are never included or excluded just because it is corporate policy, but are considered on their merits when conditions indicate they have a role to play, or conversely indicate they do not. Financial incentives are not a substitute for good management of people, but can play an important part where the circumstances are right. Where the circumstances are wrong they will just add to the costs of the business.

Appendix I

Management Check List

1. Has a thorough and objective analysis of the situation proved that it can be significantly improved by changing employee performance?
2. Has the study identified which employees?
3. Are we clear on the objectives of an incentive scheme?
4. Do we appear to have the necessary ingredients for a successful scheme as described in Chapter 3? In particular, is the employees' contribution measurable and can they determine their contribution?
5. Have all the alternatives to financial incentives been considered, e.g. improved selection, training, supervision, layout, equipment, tooling, design, materials, communication, involvement?
6. Can we design a scheme which addresses our particular problem?
7. Can we write and articulate a formula which all the affected employees will understand?
8. Will they be able to see a clear link between their efforts and earnings?
9. Have we the resources to implement and control such a scheme?
10. Have we the information systems to support the scheme?
11. Will the scheme be cost-effective in terms of increased returns and more than cover administration costs?
12. Have we allowed for changes that may be necessary to negotiate it?
13. Can we negotiate or introduce a trial period?
14. Have we worked out the costs and a plan for coping if the scheme is not successful?
15. Have we the expertise and resources to develop and implement a sound negotiation and communication plan?
16. Have we defined the role of the unions and assessed the effect of a scheme on their influence?
17. If the scheme is highly successful will we be able to market and sell the increased level of products or services?

18. Would such improved performance create problems for support areas or of facilities, inventory costs, etc?
19. Can all functions cope with any increased workload generated by the scheme?
20. Can supervision cope with the change?
21. Will any individuals or groups require training if the scheme is introduced?
22. Would the scheme cause problems of pay differentials and lead to pressure from other employees for pay increases?
23. Will the scheme have any adverse effects on employee efficiency, e.g. by increasing resistance to mobility, new technology or other changes?
24. Have we identified who will be responsible for launching and administering the scheme and assessed the workload implications?
25. Does our proposed timing allow sufficient time for negotiations, adequate communication, any training needed and administrative tasks such as redesign of systems, writing a computer programme, printing forms, etc.?
26. How does a financial incentive scheme relate to our future personnel plans and strategy?

Remember – an incentive scheme *must:*

- generate a worthwhile return to both employees and the company;
- be simple enough to be understood by employees;
- provide an incentive for all employees that need to be motivated;
- maintain the quality of the product or service (preferably improve it);
- be structured so that increased earnings are achievable by all participating employees;
- not generate conflict over the basis of payment;
- not create pressures for overmanning;
- not inhibit change.

Appendix II

An Added Value Bonus Scheme

Added value schemes which were popular during a period of Incomes Policy in the 1970s, lost their attraction in the later recession when falls in demand led to cut-backs in production capacity. The concept of added value is still frequently used, however, in educating employees about costs and output. The following is typical of schemes introduced in that earlier period, most of which have now been replaced.

An added value productivity scheme

It is agreed that a self-financing productivity scheme will be applicable to all members of signatory unions with effect from accounting period 1, 1978 in accordance with the following provisions:

(1) Departments covered by the scheme

It is intended that the scheme will apply to all staff employees of the Division.

(2) Objectives of the scheme

(a) To produce genuine improvement in the Division's productivity.
(b) To enable staff employees to share in the financial benefit of such improvement.
(c) To promote co-operation between all departments and levels in the Division.

(d) To promote the achievement and maintenance of quality standards.
(e) To operate the scheme through normal management processes and procedures and with the co-operation of union representatives and members.
(f) To promote effective consultation on the scheme's operation by providing essential production, quality, and cost data to employees and their representatives.
(g) To be self-financing and operate within the guidelines of the Government's 1977 Incomes Policy.

(3) Calculation of bonus

Productivity shall be measured by the ratio of added value to employee costs. Improvement in this ratio by comparison with its average over the preceding three years, 1975, 76 and 77, will produce 'savings' from which bonus payments will be made.

(a) *Added value (AV)*
Added value shall be calculated by:
1. Taking sales and adjusting for the change in the sales value of work in progress; and
2. Subtracting the value of the purchases of goods, materials and services consumed in producing that sales value.

(b) *Employee costs (EC)*
These are the total cost of employing staff (e.g. salaries, pensions, N.H.I., etc.).
(c) *Standard added value ratio (SR)*
This is the ratio of AV/EC for the total of the previous three years. The SR used for comparison with results in 1978 is 1.331.
(d) *The standard added value* in 1978 is therefore 1.331 × Actual EC for 1978.
(e) *Amount for distribution*
The total monies for distribution as bonus is given by:
$\frac{1}{2}$ Actual AV for the half year − Standard AV for the half year

(4) Payment of bonus

(a) Bonus shall be paid twice a year in accounting periods 7 and 13. Both of these shall be interim payments in respect of the year's results. In succeeding years, the first payment shall be adjusted to correct payment in line with audited accounts for the whole of the previous year.

(b) The total amount available (see 3(e)) shall be distributed to those in employment at the time of payment in proportion to individuals' weeks of paid employment at their basic salaries plus Phase I supplement on payroll records at the time of payment.

(5) Productivity improvements

(a) *Maintenance of quality and production standards*
It is agreed that management and members of the signatory unions shall be committed to achieve and wherever possible improve upon production targets and quality standards.

Management retain the right to adjust production schedules to meet changes in customer demand and continue its policy of raising quality standards as and when technological or design changes make this feasible, subject to the existing agreed consultative processes.

(b) *Productivity improvement – departmental and inter-departmental*
Departmental managers shall use their management structure to discuss and establish programmes and targets for productivity improvements within their own departments and inter-departmentally. These shall be treated with the same commitment to achievement and visibility as the Divisions' production targets.

(6) General

(a) A sub-committee of the Joint Divisional Consultative Committee shall be established to discuss the operation of the scheme with the aim of publicising progress and promoting the scheme's objectives.
(b) Any questions about or problems arising from the scheme's operation shall be progressed through the agreed procedure.
(c) In the event of any significant unforeseen changes in operating conditions, and in any case after 12 months' operation, the scheme shall be reviewed.
(d) There will be no staff redundancy as a direct result of the scheme.

Appendix III

BAT Industries PLC Save-As-You-Earn Share Option Scheme

BAT Industries introduced employee share option schemes in 1980, and when they revised them to take advantage of the 1984 legislation several thousand employees were already taking part. The following description has been taken from their employee booklet and is included here both as an example of a successful SAYE scheme, and as an illustration of how such schemes can be simply and clearly explained to employees. For the purpose of this example references to the company's other, non-SAYE, schemes have been deleted:

Changes in the Option Schemes

Following the 1984 Finance Act a number of changes were introduced in the Rules of the Option Schemes.

The Option Scheme

The maximum amount which may be saved was increased to £100 per month or £25 per week (from £50 per month, £12.50 per week).

Those already participating in the A Option Scheme who are saving less than £100 per month (or £25 per week) may apply for further options to bring their current savings up to this limit.

Shares and share options

Although the booklet tries to avoid using technical language, some of the terms used may be unfamiliar, so here are a few definitions:

Shares are units of ownership in a company. They are bought by people who wish to own part of the company and who then become its shareholders. If a company makes a profit it usually pays dividends to its shareholders of so much per share out of that profit.
The Stock Exchange is the market-place where shares are bought and sold. The price of the shares goes up and down according to demand and many other factors. The Stock Exchange price is shown in most newspapers.
An option is a right to buy shares at a future date, at a price which has been fixed in advance. An option is exercised when it is used to buy shares.

An employee share option scheme sets aside a number of shares in a company and gives employees options to buy those shares if they want to. Any employee who chooses to join the scheme will have an opportunity to buy shares later.

Are you eligible?

You are if

- the company you work for is a BAT Industries subsidiary which has been nominated for this purpose (referred to as a 'participating company'). Your personnel department or the Group Secretarial department will be able to tell you whether your company has been nominated; and
- you usually work for 20 hours a week or more; and
- you live in the United Kingdom and are subject to tax under Case 1 of Schedule E (which applies to all employed people who live and work in the UK apart from those in exceptional circumstances); and
- you have been continuously employed by a participating company for at least four years at the relevant qualifying date. There is to be a qualifying date each year that options are made available. It does not matter if the company you work for has been a BAT Industries subsidiary for less than four years.

If you are eligible you can apply for A options.

BUT if you will be retiring within three years, other than at your normal retirement age, there will be no point in applying for A options.

BAT Industries Employee Share Option

Each year in which options are to be granted an announcement will be made, giving:

- the number of shares available for options in that year;
- the option price;
- the closing date for applications.

Application forms will be available in plenty of time before the closing date:

GREEN ones for A options.
SAYE forms (for the A Option Scheme)

You can apply for additional options in later years if you want to, within the limits of the schemes, provided you are still an eligible employee.

When the options have been granted (and it may take some weeks to process all the applications), you will be sent an option certificate. You

The basics of the scheme

Option price	*A Options* Stock Exchange price on the specified day less ten per cent.
Limits	You decide how much you want to save each week or month. Minimum: £10 a month (£2.50 a week). Maximum: £100 a month (£25 a week).
What you do	You complete an A option application and take out a SAYE contract to save regularly for 5 years.
What you get	You are given A options to buy shares at the option price to a value equal to the amount you will have saved over 5 years.
Exercising options	After 5 years you cease saving under your SAYE contract. You take your SAYE bonus in cash and you may use all or part of the savings to buy shares at the option price.

should keep this in a safe place because it is a valuable document, and you will need it if you choose to exercise your options.

After a few years, if you wish to, you may exercise your options and buy the shares reserved for you at the option price.

A Options

The *option price* under the A Option Scheme is the Stock Exchange price of a share on the specified date (which is just before applications are made) less 10 per cent.

A options are linked to savings made through a Save-As-You-Earn contract with the Department for National Savings.

You must complete a SAYE contract in order to be granted A options. Existing contracts will not be accepted because each application for an A option must be accompanied by a new SAYE contract.

You will be granted options at the A option price up to the value of your total savings under the SAYE contract. That will be 60 times your monthly saving if you are paid monthly, or 240 times your weekly saving if you are paid weekly.

When you become entitled to a bonus on your SAYE contract you may exercise all or some of the A options and buy the shares that have been reserved for you. If you wish to exercise any of your A options you must do so within six months of the first bonus date.

When the SAYE contract comes to an end and the savings are repaid to you, if you continue to be eligible you may apply for another grant of A options when they are next made available, whether you have exercised the previous options or not. Savings under your new SAYE contract, when added to those under any SAYE contracts which have not been terminated, must not exceed the limit of £100 per month or £25 per week.

The SAYE contract

The rules of the SAYE contract are set out in the prospectus and application which you must sign and you should read them carefully. This is how it works:

You save a regular amount which must be at least £10 per month or £2.50 per week. The maximum you may save is £100 a month or £25 a week.

Your employer will deduct the savings from your pay and transfer it to the Department for National Savings (DNS) on your behalf.

Your saving will start a few months after the A options have been granted to you. You will save for 60 months or 240 weeks, after which you will be entitled to a bonus from the DNS. You then have six months following this bonus date during which you can exercise your A options. Alternatively you can allow your options to lapse and you may leave the savings with the DNS for another two years and earn a bigger bonus.

It is important to remember that the money you save under the SAYE contract is yours. You do not have to exercise the A options and you may take all your savings in cash if your prefer.

You can stop saving under the SAYE contract if you wish. To do this just tell your employer to stop making the regular deductions from your pay. If you decide to stop saving before the first bonus date you may be entitled to some interest in respect of the savings made up to that time, but it will be less than the bonus and you will not be able to exercise your A options.

The SAYE contract allows you to miss up to six months' contributions without the contract ending – but each month's contribution that you miss will have to be paid later, and will delay the bonus date by a month.

A options Save-as-you-earn for 5 years to buy shares. Option price at 10 per cent discount

Application time

The A option price is fixed: it is the Stock Exchange price of BAT Industries shares less 10 per cent

YOU DECIDE WHAT YOU CAN AFFORD TO SAVE.

How you save depends on how you are paid:

- Monthly paid-monthly saving: £10–£100 a month
- Weekly paid-weekly saving: £2.50–£25 a week
- You fill in two forms: the green: application form 'A' Option; and the Save-as-you-earn contract form.

Grant of options

Send in the forms and the Company calculates the total saved over 5 years. You will be given A options over as many BAT Industries ordinary shares at the A option price as can be bought with your 5 years' savings.

When you are granted the options you are sent the Option Certificate.

You save for 5 years

For 5 years your employer deducts the saving for you from your weekly or monthly pay and deposits it, on your behalf, with the DNS. It is still your money.

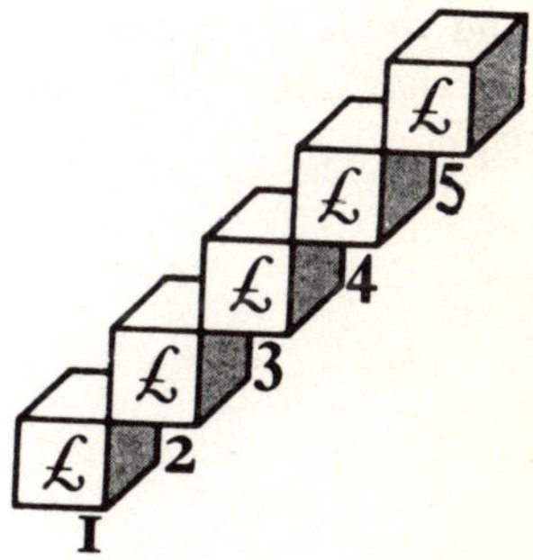

At the end of 5 years	The exercise period
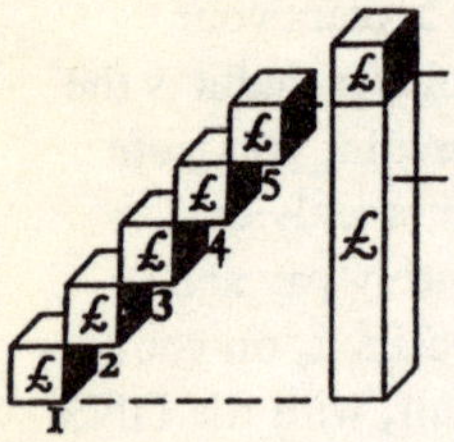 After 5 years you stop saving. The DNS gives you the TAX-FREE BONUS as well as repaying ALL YOUR SAVINGS. YOU NOW HAVE A CHOICE and you have six months to make up your mind before the options lapse.	Six months from the bonus date in which you may take BONUS and SAVINGS as  OR take BONUS as  and take SAVINGS to buy the SHARES by exercising your A OPTIONS. You will probably want to exercise your A options only if the Stock Exchange price of BAT Industries shares is higher than your option price. If it is not you would be able to buy shares more cheaply on the Stock Exchange.

Application time	Grant of options	Years 1 to 5
Suppose that BAT Industries shares were 320p on the Stock Exchange. The A option price will be fixed at 320p less 10% = 288p (that is £2.88 per share). Mr A wants to apply for A options. He has decided that he can afford to save	Mr A is given options on £1,800 worth of shares at the option price of £2.88 per share = 625 shares.	For 5 years Mr A has £30 deducted each month from his pay and paid to the DNS under his SAYE contract. All the while the Stock Exchange price of BAT Industries may be changing but the option price stays fixed at 288p.

Continuation of table

Application time	Grant of options	Years 1 to 5
£30 a month, or £7.50 a week. Over 5 years he will have saved £1,800. He sends in his option and S.A.Y.E. applications.		

End of year 5	Exercise period	
The SAYE bonus date arrives, Mr A stops saving. Mr A now has 6 months to decide on his next move.	Does Mr A want to exercise his options? He sees that the share price is now 460p (that is £4.60 per share). He decides to exercise his A options to buy 625 shares for only £2.88 each. So for the £1,800 that he saved Mr. A gets 625 shares worth £2,875. He also receives the bonus on his SAYE contract, free of tax.	Mr A is now a shareholder. He can do either of two things: (1) He can keep the shares and receive the income from dividends; or (2) He can sell them (all at once or bit by bit) and obtain cash. Of course if he does sell the shares the amount he will obtain will depend on the Stock Exchange price when he sells.

But

In all of these cases you may only exercise A options over the number of shares which can be bought with the savings made up to the date of leaving the company and in exercising the options you or your personal representatives must use the money which you withdraw from the DNS.

Except in the circumstances outlined above, A options may be exercised only during the six months following the fifth anniversary of the start of your SAYE contract which is a few months after the date when your A options were granted.

You can exercise all or just some of your A options.

The A options which you hold belong to you personally and cannot be transferred or assigned to anyone else.

Tax and A options

There is no income tax to pay on your SAYE savings when they are returned to you, nor on the bonus.

Nor will there be any income tax on your A options, either when you are granted them or when you exercise them and buy shares (except in the unlikely event of your exercising an A option because of a takeover, or voluntary liquidation of BAT Industries within 3 years of being granted the option).

If subsequently you sell the shares which you bought by exercising your A options and make a profit on them, you may have to pay capital gains tax on that profit. The liability, if any, will depend on whether you have made any other capital gains or losses that year and whether your total gain that year exceeds an annual exemption (which is normally increased each year in line with the prices index).

Notes on A options

If you leave as a result of injury, illness or redundancy, or if you retire at the age of 65 for men or 60 for women or your normal retirement age under the terms of your employment, you will have six months from the date of leaving or retiring to exercise your A options.

If you die before the SAYE Bonus date your personal representatives may exercise your A options within 12 months from your death.

If you die after the Bonus Date but within the 6 months exercise period, your personal representatives may exercise your A options within 12 months of the Bonus Date.

If you leave for any other reason, and in particular, if you retire before your normal retirement age or if the company you work for ceases to be a BAT Industries subsidiary:

- If you have held A options for over 3 years you will have 6 months in which to withdraw your savings from the DNS and exercise your A options.
- If you have not held your A options for 3 years they may not be exercised but you may continue the SAYE contract if you wish.

Appendix IV

Reed International UK and Overseas Executive Share Option Schemes (1984)

The following is a summary of the main features of the Executive Schemes ('the Schemes').

1. Constitution

The Schemes will be governed by Rules and will be administered by the Directors. The UK Executive Share Option Scheme will be submitted to the Inland Revenue for approval under the Finance Act 1984 after Royal Assent has been given.

2. Number of shares available

The maximum number of ordinary shares which may be issued under the Schemes is 6 000 000 (representing approximately 5% of the present issued ordinary share capital) but subject to adjustment in the circumstances described in paragraph 10 below. The total number of ordinary shares issued or capable of issue under the Schemes and the 1973 Executive Scheme during a ten year period will not exceed 5% of the Company's issued ordinary share capital at the end of that period. The number of ordinary shares made available to the Schemes may be further restricted to ensure that the number issued or capable of issue under the Schemes and the SAYE Scheme does not exceed 12 000 000 and that the number issued or capable of issue under all the Company's share option schemes over a ten year period does not exceed 10% of the issued ordinary share capital at the end of the period.

3. Eligibility

The Scheme will be available to such executive Directors and full-time senior employees of the Company and its subsidiaries as may from time to time be selected to participate by the Directors. No eligible employee will be entitled as of right to participate in the Schemes.

4. Offers of participation

Offers of options may be made only during the period of 30 days following the release by the Company of its interim and/or final results each year, save in the case of the first invitation which may be made when the Directors consider it appropriate.

5. Maximum individual participation

An option may not be granted to an individual selected to participate if the total subscription price thereunder would, when added to the subscription price of ordinary shares issued or capable of issue to him under options previously granted to him under the Schemes or the 1973 Executive Scheme, exceed four times his PAYE earnings, excluding benefits in kind, for that or the previous tax year in the case of the UK Scheme, or four times his annual remuneration at that time or, if higher, his remuneration and bonus and/or commission for the previous calendar year in the case of the Overseas Scheme.

6. Subscription price

The price per ordinary share at which a participant may acquire ordinary shares ('the subscription price') on the exercise of an option will be the middle market price of an ordinary share of the Company on the Stock Exchange on the day immediately preceding the date on which the option is granted, as derived from the Daily Official List, or the nominal value of an ordinary share (if greater).

7. Exercise of options

Options may normally be exercised after the expiry of three years, but before the expiry of ten years from the date of grant, but may be exercised earlier in the circumstances described in paragraph 8 below.

8. Early exercise of options and lapse of options

(i) Leaving service in special circumstances

If

(a) a participant leaves service by reason of injury, disability or redundancy; or

(b) the participant's employing company ceases to be a subsidiary of the Company or the division in which he is employed is disposed of,

then the option may be exercised during the following six months and will then lapse, unless he dies in this period (see sub-paragraph (iv) below).

(ii) Retirement

If a participant retires, his option may generally be exercised during the following two years and will then lapse. However, if retirement takes place at normal retirement age the option may only be exercised if a participant has held his option for at least eighteen months before retiring and it may not be exercised until three years from its grant.

(iii) Leaving service in other circumstances

If a participant leaves or is dismissed in circumstances other than those mentioned in (i) and (ii) above, then his option will lapse forthwith.

(iv) Death of a participant

On the death of a participant, his personal representatives will be entitled to exercise his option within the twelve months following his death, and if the option is not exercised within that period, it will lapse.

(v) Winding-up

In the event of a members' voluntary winding-up of the Company, except for the purpose of reconstruction or amalgamation, a participant may elect to be treated as if his option had been exercised immediately prior to the commencement of the winding-up. On payment of the subscription price to the liquidator, he will rank *pari passu* with other shareholders as a creditor entitled to receive the same amount, in respect of each share for which the subscription price has been paid, as is distributed to a shareholder, in respect of such shares held by him. If no such election is made the option will lapse 90 days after the commencement of the winding-up. All options will lapse on the commencement of a winding-up of the Company other than a members' voluntary winding-up.

(vi) Take-over

If, as the result of a general offer to acquire the whole of the ordinary share capital of the Company, an offeror comes to own beneficially more than 50% of such capital, outstanding options may be exercised during the six months following the later of the date of such acquisition and the date on which the offer becomes unconditional and will then lapse. If an offeror becomes entitled to acquire shares under Section 209 of the Companies Act 1948, options will lapse one month later.

Notwithstanding (i), (ii), (iv), (v) and (vi) above all options will lapse 10 years after their grant, or twelve months after the participant's death.

9. Terms of options and issue of ordinary shares

Options will be neither transferable nor assignable. The ordinary shares over which options will be granted will upon issue rank *pari passu* with all other issued ordinary shares of the Company, save that if they are issued at a time when ordinary shares of the Company are quoted on The Stock Exchange ex-dividend, ex-rights or ex any other distribution, they will not be entitled to participate in the relevant dividend, rights or other distribution.

10. Issues and reorganisations

In the event of any capitalisation issue or rights issue or any consolidation, subdivision or reduction of capital of the Company, the number, class and subscription prices of ordinary shares subject to option and the total number of shares available to the Scheme will be subject to adjustment in a manner which the Auditors of the Company confirm in writing to be fair and reasonable.

11. Amendment

The Schemes may be amended by the Directors in any way provided that:

(i) no amendment may be made which prejudices materially the rights of participants;

(ii) amendments to the following may be made only by or with the prior approval of an Ordinary Resolution of the Company:

   (a) the basis of calculation of the subscription price;

   (b) the total number of ordinary shares available to the Schemes, except as mentioned in paragraph 10 above;

   (c) the conditions governing persons who are eligible to participate;

   (d) the maximum number of shares which a participant may take up on the exercise by him of his options except as mentioned in paragraph 10 above;

   (e) the Rules governing the times when options may be granted, the transferability and adjustment of options, the periods for exercise of options, the terms on which ordinary shares are allotted, the provisions relating to the winding-up or take-over of the Company and amendment of the Schemes;

(iii) so long as the Directors determine that the UK Scheme is to be approved by the Inland Revenue under the Finance Act 1984, no amendment may be made which would prejudice approval;

(iv) notwithstanding the foregoing, amendments may be made by the Directors in order to secure or maintain such approval.

12. Termination

The Directors may at any time terminate the Schemes and in such event no further offers of participation will be made but the subsisting rights of participants will not thereby be affected. In any event, no option may be granted under the Schemes more than ten years after the adoption of the Schemes by the Company in general meeting.

13. Overseas scheme

A separate Scheme will apply to those Directors and employees who are not employed in the United Kingdom. Apart from those modifications specifically noted above the Directors may determine that the Rules shall apply with appropriate modifications and, in particular, that any options granted to executives in the United States may qualify as 'incentive stock options' and benefit from favourable tax treatment under United States legislation.

14. Tax treatment

Under the proposals in the Finance (No.2) Bill 1984 neither the grant nor the exercise of an option under the UK Scheme will give rise to an income tax charge on the participant provided that the option is exercised either following his death or not earlier than five years after it was granted and, in either case, not later than ten years after it was granted and not within three years of exercising another option under the UK Scheme or any other approved scheme. (The Government has indicated its intention of reducing from 5 years to 3 years the period which must elapse before an option may be exercised without giving rise to an income tax charge.) If an option is exercised in other circumstances the participant will be treated as in receipt of income equal to the difference between the market value of the shares acquired on exercise of the option and the subscription price paid for them under the option. A participant who exercises his option in accordance with the terms of the Scheme will acquire shares for capital gains tax purposes at the subscription price paid together with the amount, if any on which he pays income tax and will be subject to capital gains tax on their disposal in accordance with the normal rules.

Appendix V

A Production-related Bonus Scheme

Productivity payments scheme

(1) Basis of scheme

(a) The scheme is based upon Standard Hour Performance, which is a comparison of Actual Hours used per tonne of product with Standard Hours per tonne of product.
(b) The Standard Hours per tonne of product determines the Prime Labour Costs for each of our products. It is achieved when we are able to run our lines at their correct Standard Speed, with normal reject levels, the correct number of machine/line personnel and with no more downtime than is built into each standard.
(c) Total Standard Hours are determined by multiplying the tonnage of each product over a given period by its own Target Hours/Tonne and then adding all these hours together.
(d) Total Actual Hours are derived by adding up all the actual hours used by the lines in producing that same tonnage.
(e) Total Actual Hours minus Total Standard Hours determines the variance (difference) and the percentage variance is then calculated by expressing these variance hours as a proportion of the Total Standard Hours.
(f) This percentage variance, when taken from 100 per cent determines the amount of productivity payment earned for the period and indicates the performance achieved expressed as a percentage of Standard.
(g) We achieve 100 per cent of Standard when Total Actual Hours add up to the same number as Total Actual Hours, i.e. when there is no variance.
(h) The final performance for any period for any factory will be a weighted

average of the line performance within that factory, the weighting being applied through the volumes of Standard and Actual.

(i) The objective of this Scheme is to improve our current performance as much as we possibly can, with consequential benefits for employees and the Company.

(2) Production areas/payment groups

(a) The separate areas to be assessed for productivity are:

Main Plant	A Department
Main Plant	B Department
Main Plant	C Department
Main Plant	D Department
Main Plant	E Department
Satellite Plant	

(b) Process employees who undertake site rather than factory duties as their normal job will be paid on the basis of the average site performance. This includes reserve employees at the Main Plant.

(c) At the Main Plant the payment will be calculated by taking 50 per cent of the site payment and 50 per cent of the department in which the individual is working.

(3) Calculation of the bases

(a) In order to calculate the base from which we shall try to improve in each of the separate productivity areas, a record of all performances has been maintained since March 1979.

(b) These performances were in all cases calculated in accordance with the procedure agreed with the trade unions.

(c) The accumulated performances calculated for each of the areas and expressed as a percentage of Standard are:

Main Plant	83 per cent
Lincoln Plant	93 per cent

These will be the starting levels for bonus payment in each of the above separate locations.

(d) Standard Hour Performance is not equal in all our factories and these differences are reflected in the proposed payment scale.

(4) Payment calculation

(a) Company costs fluctuate at any given time according to how well we are performing. To offset these fluctuations, it is proposed that productivity payments will be based on 4-week periods.
(b) During each of these periods Total Standard and Actual Hours will be monitored in each of the separate payment areas and the performance will then be calculated in the normal way.
(c) Performance above their individual bases will attract bonus payment according to the attached scale, which is geared to reflect the importance the Company placed upon higher efficiencies.
(d) Any productivity scheme needs to be self-financing as far as possible and no bonus payment will be made to plants who fall below their individual bases.

(5) General conditions

(a) This scheme will apply to all permanent employees covered by the Company's existing wages agreement.
(b) Payment will be made for improved performances according to the attached scale.
(c) No payment will be made to any area which fails to exceed its 1979 base.
(d) Payment will be based on four week calculation periods and will be made in the form of four weekly amounts in the weeks following each calculation period.
(e) All those employed at the end of any calculation period will qualify to receive any bonus earned during the following weeks. Those leaving the Company will forfeit any bonus entitlement.
(f) Extra payment will be made for hours worked above the normal 40 hours *pro rata* to the number of extra hours worked.
(g) Part-time employees will be paid *pro rata* to their hours.
(h) Where an employee transfers from one payment area to another during the course of a calculation period, the payment he/she will receive will be that applying to the area in which he/she is employed at the end of that period.
(i) Payments will be notified and will commence as soon as practicable after the end of each calculation period.
(j) The cumulative performance will be notified to each area each week, two weeks in arrears.
(k) Performances above 100 per cent of Standard for any calculation period will attract extra payment in proportion as in 7(a) and (b) below.

(l) Each 4 week period will stand on its own for payment purposes and no 'deficit' hours will be carried forward.
(m) The existing method of establishing and reviewing Standard will remain unchanged.
(n) Only production of acceptable quality will be used in the productivity calculation.
(o) Three months' notice will be given by either side to cancel the scheme. Notice of cancellation will be on an 'all in, all out' basis.
(p) The scheme will be reviewed on an annual basis at the time of the Wage Negotiations.
(q) No change to the Scheme will take place without negotiation.

(6) Improving Standard House Performance

(a) Improved performance can be brought about in a number of ways, mostly concerning reducing unnecessary downtime, minimising reject levels/waste and maintaining correct machine/line output rates.
(b) Specific examples of improvement include:

- Giving improved attention in carrying out duties.
- Arriving on lines promptly to assist punctual start-ups, and eliminate stoppages at shift changeovers.
- Observing correct break times and restarting lines quickly.
- Reducing absenteeism which disrupts a smooth operation.
- Co-operating fully in running/attending/supplying lines to maximise production in the common interest.

(7) Payment scales

A payment scale which reflects the importance the Company attaches to higher levels of performance follows.

New bonus rates to apply from the 3rd March, 1986.

(a) *Payment scale* — *Lincoln plant*

Achievement level (percentage of Standard)	Bonus payment (40 hour week)
89	1.00
90	1.00
91	1.00
92	1.00
93	2.25
94	2.50
95	2.85
96	3.15
97	3.45
98	3.80
99	4.15
100	4.50
101	4.85
102 etc., etc.	5.25

(b) *Payment scale* — *Main plant*

Achievement level (1 per cent of Standard)	Bonus payment/40 hour week
86	0.25
87	0.50
88	0.75
89	1.05
90	1.35
91	1.65
92	1.95
93	2.25
94	2.55
95	2.85
96	3.15
97	3.45
98	3.80
99	4.15
100	4.50
101	4.85
102 etc., etc.	5.25

Index

References are to section numbers

absenteeism, 2.03, 3.01, 3.04
age scales, rate for, 1.03, 4.03
alternatives to financial incentives, 3.04
Approved Deferred Share Trust Schemes, 5.05
attitudes, 6.01, 9.09
audits, 7.04

Basic Work Data (BWD), 4.02
Bedeaux Piece Work System, 4.01
British Institute of Management, 3.04
British Insurers, Association of, 5.05
British Leyland, 2.02, 8.01

Capital gains tax, 5.05
CEGB, 9.08
Civil Service, 7.04
communications, 5.07, 6.01, 6.02
communications' policy, 3.04
competitive pay, 1.02
conditions allowances, 4.05
consolidation, 8.03

data processing staff, 9.09
demarcations, 9.02, 9.03, 9.08
Department of Employment, 1.04, 9.01
Department of Inland Revenue, 5.03
Department of National Savings, 5.05
differential piece-rates, 4.01
differentials, 1.02, 2.02, 6.04
discipline, 9.02
disputes, 4.06, 6.05

Edwardes, Sir Michael, 2.02
employee participation and involvement, 1.01, 1.04, 3.04, 5.01, 5.08, 6.01, 6.03
English China Clay, 5.01
executive earnings, 5.02
expenses, 4.05

fall-back pay, 2.02
Fawley, 9.01
flexi-time, 4.08
Ford Motor Company, 4.06, 8.01

Gant Piece-Work System, 4.01
group bonus schemes, 4.01
Group Capacity Assessment, 4.02

Halsey System, 4.01
harmonisation, 3.04, 4.08, 9.09
Hotpoint, 5.01

ICI, 5.05
Incomes Policies, 9.01, 9.02
indirect benefits of incentives, 1.04, 2.03, 6.03
indirect incentives, 1.03
indirect workers, 4.02
Industrial Society, 3.04, 6.02
Inland Revenue criteria, 5.05, 5.07
Institute of Personnel Management, 5.01, 6.02
Investment Trust Companies, Association of, 5.06

job evaluation, 1.02
John Lewis Partnership, 5.01, 5.05
joint management union initiatives, 6.01, 6.02

labour costs, 1.03, 2.01, 2.02, 2.03, 3.05, 9.04, 9.08
leaving interviews, 4.04
lump-sum buy-out, 8.03, 9.07

Maintenance Data, 4.02
maintenance workers, 3.04
management conferences, 3.04
management morale, 3.04
management objectives, 3.01
management style, 2.03, 5.01
management's role, 1.02, 1.04
Master Clerical Data, 4.02
matching (shares), 5.05

Meriden Triumph, 5.05
merit, buying out of, 8.03
merit schemes, 1.03
motivation, 1.02

National Freight Consortium, 5.05
negotiations, 2.02, 6.01, 6.05, 6.06, 8.03, 9.05
new technology, 9.06

O & M specialists, role, 1.04, 9.04
options, share, 5.06
ordinary share capital, 5.05
overnight expenses, 4.04
overtime, 1.02, 4.08, 9.02

payment by results, definitions, 1.03
Pensions Funds, National Association of, 5.06
pensions, 4.04
performance appraisal, 1.03, 3.04
planning, 6.01, 6.05, 7.01, 9.04, 9.06
Prices and Incomes Board, 2.02
Priestman Bonus Scheme, 4.01
profit related pay, 5.03
profit sharing, 5.01, 5.02, 8.03
public relations, 3.01
pyramiding, 8.03

rate-fixing, 2.04, 4.01
redundancies, 4.07, 9.06, 9.08
red circling, 8.03
Rowan system, 4.01
Rucker plan, 4.01

Sainsbury, 5.01
salesmen, 3.04
savings related share option schemes, 5.05
Scanlon plan, 4.01
Scottish Daily News, 5.05
shareholders, 5.02, 5.04, 10.01
share schemes, 5.04, 5.05
  for executives, 5.06
shift pay, 4.08
Stock Exchange Regulations, 5.05
supervisors, 2.04, 9.04, 9.06

Talbot Peugot, 8.01
target groups, 1.05, 3.02, 8.03
task forces and working parties, 1.04, 9.04
tax concessions, 5.03, 5.05, 5.06
training, 9.08
travelling time, 4.04
trial periods, 7.03
turnover of personnel, 1.02, 4.04

union attitudes, 9.08
  objectives, 6.05
  role, 6.01, 6.04, 7.02
Unit Trust Managers, Association of, 5.06

value added schemes, 4.01, 5.01
Variable Factor Programming (VFP), 4.02
Vauxhall Motors, 8.01

wages drift, 2.02, 2.03
wage structure, 1.02, 1.04, 9.02
withholding payments, 9.07
work measurement, 1.04, 2.01
works' newspaper, 6.02
work study specialist, role, 1.04, 9.04